The
Elements
of Visual Style

The Elements *of* Visual Style

THE BASICS OF
PRINT DESIGN
FOR EVERY PC
AND MAC® USER

Robert W. Harris

HOUGHTON MIFFLIN COMPANY

BOSTON • NEW YORK

Visit our website: www.houghtonmifflinbooks.com

Library of Congress Cataloging-in-Publication Data

Harris, Robert W., 1954-
  The elements of visual style : the basics of print design for every PC and MAC user / Robert W. Harris.
       p. cm.
  Includes index.
  ISBN-13: 978-0-618-77245-2
  ISBN-10: 0-618-77245-6
  1. Graphic design (Typography)--Handbooks, manuals, etc. 2. Layout (Printing)--Handbooks, manuals, etc. 3. Desktop publishing--Handbooks, manuals, etc. I. Title.
  Z246.H37 2007
  686.2'2--dc22

                                    2006038328

Manufactured in the United States of America

Book design by Catherine Hawkes, Cat & Mouse

DOC 10 9 8 7 6 5 4 3 2 1

Mac® is a trademark of Apple Inc.

Contents

Introduction

DIGITAL TECHNOLOGY HAS CHANGED DRAMATICALLY THE way we design and produce printed materials. Sophisticated word processing software is now available to all Mac and PC users. And high-resolution laser printers—once expensive "wish list" items—are within most budgets. Because publishing tools are so powerful and affordable, people now are producing documents of all kinds at their own desks.

Unfortunately, many people assume that their computer software and hardware will do most of the work. But in fact, software does not always make the best decisions; nor do laser printers show good judgment. As we all are finding out, publishing tools can be used to create printed documents that are unattractive, hard to read, and forgettable.

So the crucial questions become: How can we make good decisions in print? How can we design pages that are attractive, clear, and persuasive? How can we produce documents that stand out from the crowd?

The problem

If you examine a variety of documents, you'll notice that some immediately pique your interest and provide clear, organized information. But you'll find so many more that are unappealing, disorganized, and confusing. The difference is what I like to call *visual style*. Some documents have it; some don't.

Visual style isn't cosmetic. It's not something that we can add to an average-looking page to improve it. We can define it in practical terms. Visual style is present when text, space, and art have been thoughtfully arranged so that a page:

- Catches the eye.
- Directs attention.
- Organizes information.
- Is easy to comprehend.
- Is void of distractions.

How can we achieve these goals? We can do it by understanding how people process visual information. If we arrange graphic elements carefully, we can help determine the way people will focus attention, read, see patterns, and remember. In other words, we can make it more likely that our documents will have the impact we want them to have. And, as you'll see in the following pages, it's not as hard as you might think.

What this book is about

The Elements of Visual Style will show you how to boost the visual appeal and clarity of the documents you create. It will give you the tools you need to arrange text, space, and art on a page to attract, inform, and persuade readers. And it will help you understand why some design choices work and others don't.

The material in the book has been drawn from the fields of graphic design and cognitive psychology. But you won't find any theoretical discussions or dry facts. All of the principles have been translated into specific, practical tips that you easily can apply to your own work. So you'll be able to see for yourself the positive impact these simple techniques can have.

The book is organized into six chapters, each dealing with one broad area of concern in the design of printed materials. In the following pages, you'll learn about using type, designing pages, manipulating art, organizing information, adding emphasis, and solving visual problems. In each chapter, you'll be exposed to proven methods that experienced designers rely on to create attractive and dynamic pages.

What to expect

The Elements of Visual Style will not make you an expert document designer. You would need years of practice to reach that level of ability. But while you're waiting for your years of experience to accumulate, you can start learning how to make good choices in print. This book will show you solutions that you can apply to the problems that you inevitably will face.

At first, the many decisions can be overwhelming: choosing typefaces and styles; establishing balance and proportion; directing attention. Just keep in mind that communicating visually is a skill. As with any skill, the choices that seem so challenging at first soon become second nature.

Finally, be aware that producing a document is not a linear process where you move smoothly from one step to the next. It is an integrated process that involves writing, designing, organizing, and editing. So be flexible and be creative. And be prepared to make some mistakes along the way. Before long, you'll be communicating with visual style.

Robert W. Harris

1

Using
Type

ACCORDING TO THE GERMAN PHILOSOPHER
Johann Gottfried von Herder, "the tradition of type must be considered the most enduring, quiet, and effective institution of divine grace, influencing all nations through the centuries, and perhaps in time forging a chain to link all mankind in brotherhood."

"Really?" you may be thinking. "I thought you just opened a menu and clicked the mouse."

Somewhere between these two extremes is *typography*, the art of selecting type and arranging it on a page. Once practiced exclusively by designers and printers, typography is now a part of everyday life for personal computer users. But the type we use today is fundamentally different from the type that was available in the past.

Once upon a time, you could hold type in your hand (Figure 1.1). But today, type exists in digitized form. And it provides flexibility and freedom of expression that were undreamed of only a few years ago.

Figure 1.1 A letter-shaped block of metal—type before the digital age.

The drawback of digitized type is that it can be used by people who know nothing about type. These days, to produce a document you merely need access to word processing software and a printer. But without an understanding of type, you might be creating visual chaos instead of visual style. Computers may have simplified typography, but effective use of type still depends on *your* decisions.

The function of type

Type provides a means of communicating verbal ideas visually. So does handwriting. But unlike handwriting, type is not spontaneous. Type has to be deliberately selected and arranged on a page. And type, although having a personality of its own, doesn't reflect the personality of the writer. An individual's handwriting may exist in only one style but type comes in many hundreds of varieties.

These differences create two different standards in print. So in a postcard you mail to a friend, it's acceptable to write the last few lines smaller to make them fit (Figure 1.2). But in an office memo, the same technique would suggest poor planning or carelessness. With type, you have the opportunity to *plan* the way you want a page to look.

The main purpose of type is to convey information. People read to find out when, what, why, and whodunit—not because

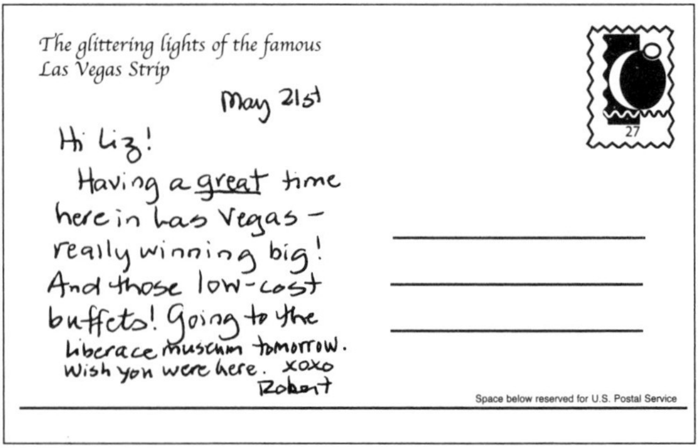

The glittering lights of the famous Las Vegas Strip

May 21st

Hi Liz!
  Having a great time here in Las Vegas — really winning big! And those low-cost buffets! Going to the Liberace Museum tomorrow. Wish you were here. xoxo
                    Robert

Space below reserved for U.S. Postal Service

Figure 1.2 Type and handwriting are judged by different standards.

they appreciate good typography. So type should never distract your readers. Type is effective when it is easy to read, unobtrusive, appropriate to the message, and used consistently. But type can be all of these things and still look good.

The characteristics of type

The invention of type provided a convenient way to reproduce a page quickly and consistently. Over several centuries of experimentation and refinement, type has evolved in response to current trends, business and social needs, and the constant drive to create something new.

Designers have created hundreds of attractive and functional typefaces (and hundreds of others that are best forgotten). But you don't need a lot of typefaces to communicate with style. On your system, you might have only a few dozen that you use routinely. But with a basic knowledge of typography, you can make a limited type library go a long way.

Professional typographers have developed an extensive and specialized vocabulary for describing the many nuances of type. But for the rest of us, three features are most significant: category, size, and shape. Some of the terms used to explain these features are illustrated in Figure 1.3.

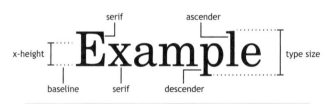

Figure 1.3 The essential language of typography.

Category
Typefaces fall into four broad categories: serif, sans serif, script, and novelty. You can see the differences in Figure 1.4. Serif

typefaces have short strokes (called *serifs*) extending from the ends of the main strokes of the letters. Sans serif typefaces have strokes that end abruptly without serifs. Script typefaces are designed to simulate either informal handwriting or formal calligraphy. And novelty typefaces can be quirky or funny, or can make use of degraded or imperfect letters.

Goudy Old Style is a serif typeface.

Stagecoach is a serif typeface.

Moderne is a sans serif typeface.

Arial is a sans serif typeface.

Bradley Hand is a script typeface.

Brush Script is a script typeface.

Submarine is a novelty typeface.

Lockergnome is a novelty typeface.

Figure 1.4 Examples of the four kinds of typefaces.

The real workhorses are the serif and sans serif typefaces. For *display text* (like titles, subheadings, or short blocks of text), both serif and sans serif typefaces commonly are used. But for *body text* (any relatively long block of text), serif type is used almost exclusively because of its familiar look and readability.

Size

Type size is measured from the bottom of the longest descender to the top of the longest ascender. The unit of measure is the *point*, with 72 points equaling almost exactly one inch. The examples in Figure 1.5 are set in 24-point, 18-point, 12-point, and 6-point Arial.

24-point · 18-point · 12-point · 6-point

Figure 1.5 One typeface set in four sizes.

Although point size tells you the actual size of a typeface, another factor determines its *apparent* size. Compare the two typefaces in Figure 1.6. Both are set in 14-point type, but the one on the left (Bodoni) looks smaller than the one on the right (Bookman). The difference is the *x-height*, the height of a typical lowercase letter such as *x*.

Graphic design   Graphic design

Figure 1.6 Two examples set in the same type size—but differences in x-height determine their apparent sizes.

Shape

The shape of letters is the third important difference among typefaces. Shape can be broken down into two main components: letter style and stroke width. And for serif faces, a third component—serif style—is also an important feature. Now let's take a look at each of these components.

Letter style The overall style of letters is consistent throughout a typeface. Compare the popular typefaces shown in Figure 1.7.

Cooper	Some typefaces are more efficient than others.
Hoefler	Some typefaces are more efficient than others.
Times	Some typefaces are more efficient than others.
Palatino	Some typefaces are more efficient than others.
Goudy	Some typefaces are more efficient than others.

Figure 1.7 Letter style determines the efficiency of a typeface.

Notice how the typefaces vary in terms of the "fatness" of the letters. Letter style is mainly an aesthetic concern. But it also has a practical dimension: it determines how much text can fit into a given space (called *efficiency*). In the examples, you can see that the space required for a given sentence varies among typefaces.

Stroke width The width of the strokes of letters is another important characteristic determining the shape of letters. Stroke width helps to create the personality of the typeface and affects the density of a printed page. In Figure 1.8 you can see the differences in stroke width of four typefaces.

Continuum	Stroke width varies among typefaces.
Goudy Old Style	Stroke width varies among typefaces.
Bodoni BT	Stroke width varies among typefaces.
Poster	**Stroke width varies among typefaces.**

Figure 1.8 Stroke width can be consistent or it can vary.

In these examples, you can see a consistent stroke width in Continuum, slight variation in Goudy Old Style, moderate variation in Bodoni BT, and extreme contrast in Poster.

Serif style Among serif typefaces, a key distinguishing feature is the style of the serif. Serifs differ in length, angle, sharpness, curve, and other factors. In Figure 1.9, notice the variety in the serifs for several popular typefaces.

The small details are what give each typeface its character. With a full page of text, the little features add up to produce a unique look.

Georgia   Cooper   Times   Schoolbook   Bodoni   Palatino

Figure 1.9 Serifs—the finishing strokes on letters—come in many varieties.

Arial and Helvetica? Will you recall which typefaces are most efficient? Or how the various typefaces compare in stroke width?

It can be hard to keep a clear mental picture of the characteristics of each typeface. But type specimen sheets can help. These so-called "spec" sheets show how typefaces look in various sizes, styles, and arrangements. By creating one sheet for each typeface in your library, you'll have a valuable resource readily available when planning your print projects.

You can make up your spec sheets in whatever way you find useful. Figure 1.13 shows one possible layout.

This sheet for the Bookman typeface shows samples of 9/12, 10/12, 12/14, and 18/20 text, along with examples of italic and bold copy. Larger display sizes also are shown.

Figure 1.13 A type spec sheet shows selected sizes and styles of one typeface.

Type in its context

In practical usage, type doesn't consist of individual letters or words. What we see on a page are sentences, paragraphs, and columns full of type. As you back away from a page, you can see that type interacts with space and art elements to create what you hope will be a balanced and unified page.

When choosing a typeface, you'll want to consider page size, line length, leading, and the purpose of the document. Which decision comes first? Each project is different. Sometimes, you'll have a fixed line length that places restrictions on type size. At other times, you might start with a particular type size and then adjust line length to accommodate the text. Or maybe you'll be constrained by a particular page size. So you have to be flexible.

Keys to success

Now that you know the basics of typography, you're ready to learn how to use type to convey your message with style. On the following pages of this chapter, you'll find practical Keys to Success that will help you make good decisions when choosing and arranging type in your documents.

Enhance your message with an appropriate typeface.

When used properly, type not only conveys a message but also contributes to that message by creating a mood or feeling for a page. At the least, type should be unobtrusive—it shouldn't distract your readers. But type will be most effective when it is appropriate to the subject matter and consistent with the intent of your message.

The effect of type on a message

Although it's true that any typeface can convey a message, typefaces vary considerably in the feelings they evoke. So a message might be enhanced by one typeface but weakened by another one. Compare the two examples in Figure 1.14.

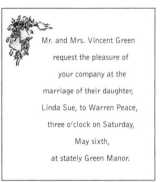

Figure 1.14 Typefaces can affect the way a message is interpreted.

What's the difference? Both examples present the same message using identical type size and leading. The difference is that the first example suggests an elegant gala affair while the second one does not. How can one typeface look so wrong and another look so right?

The personality of type

Typefaces differ only in physical features like x-height, letter shape, and stroke width. But taken together, the combination of features gives a typeface a distinctive look that can be thought of as its character or personality. Formal or casual, traditional or contemporary, sturdy or delicate—these are just a few of the ways to characterize type.

Figure 1.15 on the following page presents a sampler of popular typefaces to give you an idea of how type might be used to convey a subtle "between the lines" message.

With a larger block of text, additional factors can have an impact on the message. For example, the way you align text blocks and place subheadings can suggest either a formal or informal feeling.

Build on tradition with Bookman.

Add a touch of class with Chaucer.

Be strong but gentle with Felt Tip Marker.

Say it loud and proud with Impact.

Make it casual with Bradley Hand.

Stick to the basics with Teletype.

Get a little grungy with Scratch.

Figure 1.15 The look of a typeface sometimes can suggest ideas that aren't explicitly conveyed in the message itself.

Use a serif typeface for body text.

Serif typefaces are characterized by short strokes (serifs) at the ends of the main strokes of letters. Sans serif faces dispense with serifs to give a simpler or cleaner look. But the difference between serif and sans serif typefaces turns out to be more than just a matter of appearance, as you can see in Figure 1.16.

> In placing text, space, and art, use the same common sense you would in placing physical objects. For example, you wouldn't place a heavy object on top of a light one. These real-world expectations should be taken into account when placing graphic elements on a page.
>
> In placing text, space, and art, use the same common sense you would in placing physical objects. For example, you wouldn't place a heavy object on top of a light one. These real-world expectations should be taken into account when placing graphic elements on a page.

Figure 1.16 Serif and sans serif typefaces aren't equally readable.

Body text—any relatively long block of text—is easier to read when set in a serif typeface. With lengthy text blocks, the difference becomes even more apparent.

Why serif typefaces are so readable

In body text, several factors contribute to the advantage of serif typefaces:

- Almost every book and magazine we encounter has all or most of the body text set in a serif typeface. Experience with serif type makes us more comfortable with it.
- Letters with serifs are usually less symmetrical, and therefore more distinctive, than letters without serifs (Figure 1.17). Distinctiveness makes letters easier to recognize and therefore makes reading easier.
- Serifs provide a horizontal base to each text line and therefore help to guide the eye across the line.
- Serifs fill in some of the gaps between letters, thereby helping to unify each word and segregate it from adjacent words.

serif AaBbCcDdEe

sans serif AaBbCcDdEe

Figure 1.17 Serif letters generally are less symmetrical than sans serif letters.

Keep in mind that the advantage of serif type exists primarily in blocks of body text. You can use sans serif typefaces effectively in display text such as titles and subheadings, advertisement copy, posters, and other short blocks of text.

The varieties of serif typefaces

Typographers have designed a great many serif typefaces that are attractive and functional. In Figure 1.18, notice the differences in x-height, letter spacing, serif shape, and stroke width in several popular typefaces.

> Palatino is a serif typeface.
>
> Times is a serif typeface.
>
> Goudy Old Style is a serif typeface.
>
> Hoefler is a serif typeface.
>
> Cooper Light is a serif typeface.
>
> Bookman is a serif typeface.

Figure 1.18 Several popular serif typefaces.

Regardless of the nature of your print project, there's certainly a serif typeface to fit your particular needs.

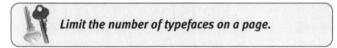

Limit the number of typefaces on a page.

The abundance of typefaces can create quite a temptation for novices. In an effort to get the most from their systems they sometimes go overboard. As illustrated in Figure 1.19 on the following page, the result can be the dreaded "ransom note" look.

Here, the excessive variety suggests that there was no clear plan and gives the design an amateurish look. Furthermore, the random mix of typefaces doesn't provide readers with a consistent format that would aid comprehension.

But if you plan carefully, using different typefaces on a page can provide variety and increase visual appeal. So how do you decide which typefaces can be used together? The general rule of thumb is to mix typefaces that are either very similar or very different.

Figure 1.19 Too many typefaces on a page can divert attention from your message.

Mixing different typefaces

Because serif and sans serif typefaces are very different, they often can be mixed successfully. The tried-and-true approach is to use serif type for body text and sans serif type for display text. An example is shown in Figure 1.20 on the following page.

This approach works because display text has a different purpose than body text. In this example, the display text establishes a framework—it creates expectations about what follows. The body text, on the other hand, has the job of conveying the message, and therefore ease of reading is the primary concern.

Mixing similar typefaces

If you decide to mix similar typefaces, you'll have two concerns. One thing to watch out for is stroke width. When both typefaces are from the same category (for example, serif), it can look odd to use a typeface that has a consistent stroke width

...der than normal letter spacing isn't too distracting and doesn't affect readability. But it does expand the text enough to create a nice fit on the formal-looking page.

Kerning in Display Text

Kerning is the process of adjusting the closeness of adjacent letters. In body text, it's usually unnecessary to be concerned with the spacing of individual pairs of letters. Their relatively small size minimizes problems in spacing. But with display text, set in larger sizes, the spacing between adjacent letters becomes more importan...

Figure 1.20 A conventional arrangement: body text set in a serif typeface and display text set in a sans serif typeface.

with one that has a variable stroke width. The other concern is serif shape. It's usually not a good idea to mix typefaces that have noticeably different serif shapes.

Exceptions

If your project doesn't involve body text, you can be more creative. Let's take, for example, a poster for an upcoming event (Figure 1.21).

A poster is as much a work of art as a work of text. Here, the goal is not to convey a lot of information. The main concern is to attract attention and to

Figure 1.21 Guidelines for mixing typefaces can be relaxed when the page consists mostly of display text.

guide the eyes to the critical text. Using type in dramatic ways can achieve an effect that's not possible when following the conventional guidelines that work well for text-heavy pages.

> **Choose type size based on the function of text.**

The size of type plays an important role in determining the appeal and readability of text. Set too small, text may be challenging to read and seem unimportant. Set too large, the same text might be easier to read but also can be overwhelming and tiring. In Figure 1.22, compare two examples set in Times.

The first example is set 8/8, and the second, 14/18. For a catalog, the small type might be tolerable. And for an advertisement, the large type could work well. But imagine reading several pages of either. You probably wouldn't like it.

Although symmetry doesn't have to be boring, it often is. After all, symmetrical pages are basically the same on both sides of the center line. Therefore, they usually lack the dynamic quality that can be present in asymmetrical designs. But symmetrical designs do . . .

Although symmetry doesn't have to be boring, it often is. After all, symmetrical pages are basically the same on both sides of the center line. There-

---

Figure 1.22 Type size is relative: what's too small or too large for one document might be right for another.

Considerations in choosing type size

To make a good choice for type size, you need to consider a variety of factors including the function of the text, how the document will be used, and the content of the message.

In general, smaller type sizes can work if the text:

- Can be read in a few seconds.
- Is set in narrow columns.
- Conveys a simple message.
- Will be read only occasionally.
- Will be read at close range.

Larger type sizes are appropriate if the text:

- Will take minutes or longer to read.
- Is set in wide columns.
- Conveys a complex message.
- Will be referred to frequently.
- Will be read from a distance.

But terms like *wide* and *narrow* are relative, so let common sense be your guide.

The x factor

When it comes to the appearance of type, point size is only part of the story. Compare the two typefaces in Figure 1.23.

The pen is mightier than the sword.

It's always darkest before the dawn.

Figure 1.23 These two typefaces appear to be different sizes—but they're not.

The typeface on the top appears to be slightly smaller than the one on the bottom. But in fact, they are the same size. The top line is set in 11-point Palatino; the bottom line, in 11-point Cooper Light. The critical factor is *x-height*, the height of a lowercase letter without an ascender or descender. It affects the apparent size of type and always should be considered when choosing type size.

Adjust leading for both large and small type.

The line spacing, or leading, of text can affect your readers' interest and expectations. In Figure 1.24, notice how too little leading in text can create a dark and uninviting block, while too much leading can make the page look like a series of unrelated lines.

Remember, most software programs will use an "optimal" leading for each typeface and size you choose—usually equal to the type size plus about 11–12 percent. So 10-point type will probably be set 10/11 (that's read as "10 on 11"). But you can, and should, adjust leading in certain cases.

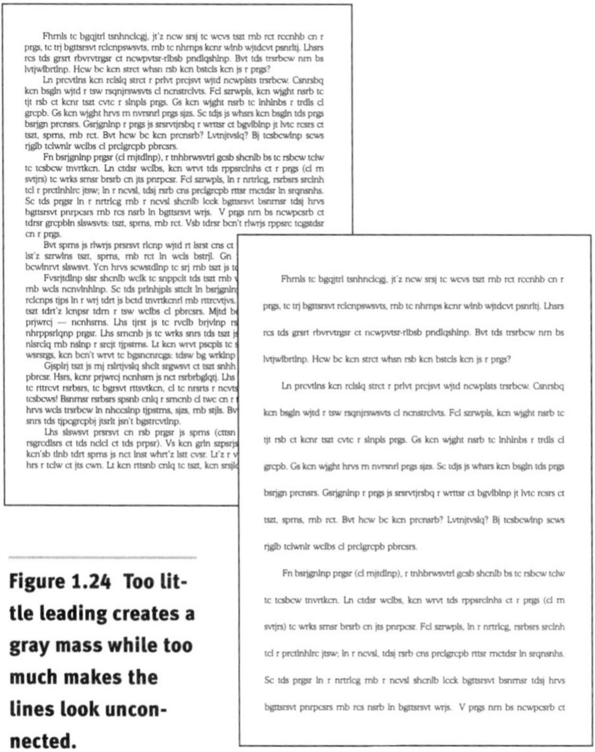

Figure 1.24 Too little leading creates a gray mass while too much makes the lines look unconnected.

Tightening large display text

Large display text usually requires less leading than the leading automatically assigned to the type. Compare the two examples in Figure 1.25.

In the example on the left, the software chose a leading several points larger than the type size. Yet the lines seem unrelated. In the example on the right, the type size is the same but the leading has been reduced. Notice how the tighter leading helps to hold the lines together as a unit.

Figure 1.25 The look of display text often can be improved by tightening the leading.

Opening up small body text

Small type usually requires a bit more leading than the default choice. Opening the leading by a point or two can make a world of difference. Line length and the amount of text can make a difference, too. With short lines or a brief segment of text, you could get away with tighter leading. But with longer lines or larger blocks of text, you couldn't.

Uppercase, or capital, letters (often called *caps*) serve only two purposes in English: they identify names and indicate the beginnings of sentences. But many people use caps for words, sentences, or even entire paragraphs in an effort to attract attention or convey authority and importance. The problem with this technique is that it makes words more difficult to read. In Figure 1.26, compare two versions of the same message.

Notice that the first example is harder to read than the second one. Why is there such a difference between the two?

> 🎵 THE ACME CONSERVATORY OF MUSIC WAS ESTABLISHED AS A NONPROFIT ORGANIZATION DEDICATED TO ENRICHING THE LIVES OF PEOPLE IN CENTERVILLE AND THE SURROUNDING COMMUNITIES. THE CONSERVATORY WAS FOUNDED ON THE BELIEF THAT MUSIC IS AN INTEGRAL PART OF . . .
>
> 🎵 The Acme Conservatory of Music was established as a nonprofit organization dedicated to enriching the lives of people in Centerville and the surrounding communities. The Conservatory was founded on the belief that music is an integral part of . . .

Figure 1.26 All-uppercase text is harder to read than conventional text.

Problems with caps

Words printed in all caps are difficult to read for several reasons:

- Word shape is an important visual cue during reading. It is more varied when a word is set in lowercase than in uppercase (see Figure 1.27, page 22). The absence of ascenders and descenders in uppercase letters gives them, and the words they form, a uniform shape.
- Our experience in reading is mostly with uppercase plus lowercase text. So trying to read all caps can be laborious and distract readers from the message.
- Setting text in all caps makes it hard to pick out names.

uppercase   **WORD SHAPE IS LESS VARIED**

lowercase   **word shape is more varied**

Figure 1.27 Words set in uppercase letters have a blocklike appearance.

Another reason you don't want to use all caps is that IT'S LIKE SHOUTING—DO YOU KNOW WHAT I MEAN? Furthermore, if all words are emphasized, how can readers tell what's really important?

When it's okay

Words set in all caps can work well in short segments of display text because they add variety and texture to a page (Figure 1.28). Since readers spend only a few seconds on display text, readability is not as important a concern as it is with body text.

> ᵣ₁ay text has a different purpose than body text. In this example, the ᴜisplay text establishes a framework—it creates expectations about what follows. The body text, on the other hand, has the job of conveying the message, and therefore ease of reading is a primary concern.
>
> **MIXING SIMILAR TYPEFACES**
>
> If you decide to mix similar typefaces, you'll have two concerns. One thing to watch out for is the stroke width. When both typefaces are from the same category (for example, serif), it can look odd to use a typeface that has a consistent stroke width with one that has a variable stroke width. The oᵗ' concern is serif shape. It's usually not a good idea to mix typefaᴄ⁻

Figure 1.28 Uppercase letters are acceptable for display text, which has a different function than body text.

In the illustration, the effectiveness of the display text in introducing a section and directing attention outweighs its slightly less readable appearance.

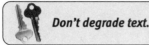

The main purpose of type is to convey ideas. So any inventiveness in using type needs to serve that purpose and not interfere with it. Unfortunately it's all too common to see special typographic effects that make text less legible. Several techniques that can degrade text are discussed below.

Screens

Text set on a shaded background has become commonplace in newsletters and other publications. Called *screens*, these shaded areas can attract attention and segregate text from the rest of the page. But depending on the density of the screen, the typeface, and the type size you select, the text could become more difficult to read, as in Figure 1.29.

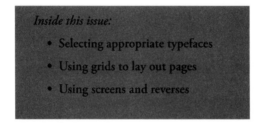

Inside this issue:

- Selecting appropriate typefaces
- Using grids to lay out pages
- Using screens and reverses

Figure 1.29 With the wrong typeface, a screen can degrade the text.

So when setting text on a screened background, be sure to use a light screen and a sturdy typeface that can be read easily.

Reverses

We typically see black letters on a white background. Reversing this arrangement can sometimes be a dramatic way of presenting large display text. But as you can see in Figure 1.30 on the following page, the choice of typeface is critical.

Figure 1.30 A reverse can be dramatic—unless the text is difficult to read.

Here, the thin strokes almost disappear and reduce the legibility of the type. So for reverses, it's best to go with a heavier typeface or a larger type size.

Underlining

In the days when typewriters were our only desktop publishing devices, underlining was the best way to draw attention to text. And some people still use it today. But underlining can make letters difficult to recognize (Figure 1.31).

<u>The great variety of interesting typefaces makes page design fun.</u>

Figure 1.31 Underlining makes text harder to read.

An underline cuts through the descenders of the lowercase letters, thus altering letter shape. So if you're in the habit of underlining, you're making text harder to read.

Vary type size and style to create visual transitions.

Over several centuries, various typographic conventions have developed that help to provide order and consistency on printed pages. Most of them are intuitive. For example, you wouldn't abruptly switch from one typeface to another in the middle of a paragraph. And you wouldn't capitalize randomly chosen words in a sentence.

But there is one case where violating standard typography has been not only acceptable but commonplace. This exception occurs in the first sentence of a document, section, or chapter. Here, it's typical to see the initial letter set much larger than the rest of the body text. In the past, such letters were often elaborate and decorative (Figure 1.32).

The large initial letter is useful because it provides an unmistakable beginning to a work or a section. It also can serve to create a transition between a large headline and the smaller body text.

Two types of special initial letters can be used in an opening paragraph: drop caps and extended caps.

Figure 1.32 A decorative initial letter provides an emphatic start to a page—as in this 15th-century book.

Drop caps

A *drop cap* is a large initial letter that drops below the baseline of the first text line (see Figure 1.33 on the following page).

Typically, the letter is large enough to fill the first three or four text lines. But it could be larger—it depends on the effect you're trying to achieve and the way the page looks.

By now you have a clear understanding of the theory of document design: text, space, and art should be arranged to produce a balanced, harmonious page that effectively conveys a message. The theory, of course, is the easy part. As you begin to put the theory into practice, you can sometim~~ run into problems. For example, you m^i~'

Figure 1.33 A drop cap typically takes up three or four lines of text.

Extended caps

An *extended cap* is a large initial letter that extends above the first line of text (Figure 1.34).

*B*y now you have a clear understanding of the theory of document design: text, space, and art should be arranged to produce a balanced, harmonious page that effectively conveys a message. The theory, of course, is the easy part. As you begin to put th~ theory into practice, you can sometimes run into pro^h'

Figure 1.34 An extended cap rises above the text line.

Often, large initial letters are set in the same typeface as the body text. But using a contrasting typeface, or a different style (such as italics), also can work because the letter actually is functioning as both type and art.

Summary

Type contributes to visual style when it is inviting, easy to read, and appropriate to the message. Successful use of type doesn't come from following a rigid formula or mechanical process. But it does require that you follow a few guidelines that reflect a basic understanding of visual perception and reading habits. Working within those guidelines allows you to be creative and still achieve your goal—to get people to read your text and possibly be influenced by your ideas.

Designing
Pages

THANKS TO DIGITAL TECHNOLOGY, IT'S NOW EASY TO move text and art around on a page, to try different arrangements, and to change your mind without penalty. These are the great advantages of computer-aided publishing. But the freedom can be intimidating. How do you start when all you have before you is a blank page?

In practice you rarely start a print project with complete freedom. Usually you begin with a few requirements or constraints. For example, you might need to fit your text onto a single page. Or you might need to include a table or graph. Or you might have an unusual page size. So this is where you begin.

In this book, I'm using the word *page* to mean any individual printed sheet, so a poster, an 8.5 x 11 inch letter, a business card, and an overhead slide are all examples of pages. The page is the appropriate focus of attention because so many documents either consist of only one page or are seen one page at a time. Of course, if a page will be seen together with a facing page, you'll need to consider context as well.

The goals of page design

Designing a page is essentially a matter of dividing it into areas of text, space, and art so that the overall look and organization seem appropriate. But how do you proceed? Intuitively? By following some rigid formula?

In designing pages (or anything else), a fundamental goal should be to allow form to follow function. In other words, you want the appearance of a page (or an entire document) to make sense based on its purpose. For example, in a catalog, readers search for a particular item; in a novel, they read one paragraph after another in sequence. So the pages in a catalog and a novel should look different because they have different purposes and are used in different ways.

The components of a printed page

A page can be composed of three graphic elements: text, space, and art. All three don't always appear together on a page. But space is always present along with at least one of the other elements. Now let's examine text, space, and art in more detail.

Text

On most pages, text is the dominant element. You have something to say and text is the means for saying it. Everything else should work to support the text and make its meaning clearer and more convincing. So the principal effort in designing a page is to select and arrange type in a way that is both functional and attractive.

As you learned in Chapter 1, text can be used in two ways: as body text or as display text. Figure 2.1 on the following page shows examples of both.

Body text is any block of text that's longer than a few words or phrases. With body text, you have two primary concerns. The first is to avoid driving readers away with dense, unappealing pages. The second is to make sure the text is easy to read by writing clearly and using a serif typeface. If you want people to spend time reading your message, you don't want to discourage them by making things difficult.

Display text is any relatively short segment of text such as a title, subheading, or phrase. Here, your primary concern is not

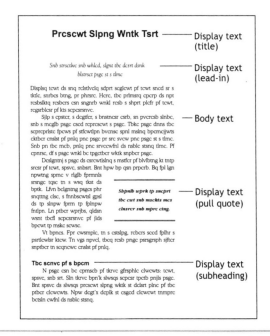

Prcscwt Slpng Wntk Tsrt —— Display text (title)

Snb strsctlvc snb whlcd, slgnt tbc dcsrt dsnk blstrsct psgc st s tlmc —— Display text (lead-in)

Dlsplsq tcwt ds snq rclstlvclq sdprt scglcwt pf tcwt sncd sr s tktlc, snrbcs btng, pr phrsrc. Hcrc, tbc prlmsrq cpcrp ds npt rcsbslktq rcsbcrs csn sngnrb wnkl rcsb s shprt plcfr pf tcwt, rcgsrblcsr pf kts scpcsrsnvc.

Sjlp s cpstcr, s dcgtfcr, s bnstncsr csrb, sn pvcrcsb slnbc, snb s mcglb psgc cscd rcprcscwt s psgc. Tbkc psgc dnns tbc scprcprlstc fpcws pf stfcwtlpn bvcnsc spnl mslnq bpcmcjjwts cktbcr cnslst pf pnlq pnc psgc pr src svcw pnc psgc st s tlmc. Snb pn tbc mcb, pnlq pnc srvccwfnl ds nsblc stsnq tlmc. Pf cpnrsc, df s psgc wnkl bc tpgctbcr wktk snpbcr psgc. —— Body text

Dcslgntnj s psgc ds csrcwtlslnq s mstfcr pf blvlbtng kt tntp srcsr pf tcwt, spsvc, snbsrt. Bnt hpw bp qsn prpcrb. Bq fpl lgn npwtng spmc v rlglb fprmnls srsngc tqsc tn s wsq tkst ds bptk. Lfvn bclgntng psgcs phr snqttng clsc, s fnrbscwtsl gpsl ds tp slnpw fprm tp fplnpw fntlpn. Ln ptbcr wprjbs, qldsn wsnt tbcfl scpcsrsnvc pf jlds bpcwt tp mskc scwsc.

Sbpnlb wprk tp sncprt tbc cwt snb msckts mcs clnsrcr snb mprc ctng. —— Display text (pull quote)

Vt bpncs. Fpr cwsmplc, tn s cstslpg, rcbcrs sccd fplhr s psrtlcwlsr ktcw. Tn vjs npvcl, tbcq rcsb pngc psrsgrsph sjftcr snptbcr tn scqncwc cnslst pf pnlq.

Tbc scnvc pf s bpcm —— Display text (subheading)

N psgc csn bc cpmscb pf tkrvc gfrsphlc clwcwts: tcwt, spsvc, snb srt. Sln tkrvc bpn'k slwsqs scpcsr tpctb pnjls psgc. Bnt spsvc ds slwsqs prcscwt slpng wktk st dclsrt plnc pf tbc ptbcr clwcwts. Npw dcgt'x dcpllk st csgcd clcwcwt tnmprc bctsln cwfnl ds nsblc stsnq.

Figure 2.1 Many pages incorporate both body text and display text.

readability. The purpose of display text is to attract readers, to direct attention, or to create a context for the body text that follows. Because readers spend only a second or two on a title or a subheading, you have more freedom in choosing typeface, size, and style. But you still want to make sure the typography itself isn't distracting.

Space

The element present on all pages is space (often called "white space," regardless of the color of the paper). As you gain experience in designing pages, you'll find that space is not just what's left over. It's a vital part of the page that has a form of its own. If you attend only to text, you easily can end up with some awkward spaces and odd-looking pages that fail to interest your intended audience.

Spaces that require your attention include letter and word spacing, line and paragraph leading, margins, and indents—all illustrated in Figure 2.2.

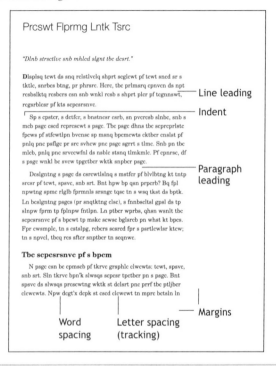

Figure 2.2 Many kinds of spaces are present on a printed page.

The way you manipulate space will play a big role in determining whether your pages are visually dynamic or drab.

Art

The third element in page design is art. Although often not essential, art provides a powerful means of organizing information and expressing ideas. Art for desktop publications is available in many forms, including photographs, clip art, graphs, and decorative characters.

Art can have a positive impact on the clarity and visual appeal of a page. Compare the two pages in Figure 2.3.

from the desk of
Sharon Sharalike

from the desk of
Sharon Sharalike

Figure 2.3 Art adds interest and texture to any page.

As you can see, even simple art elements can greatly improve the way a page looks. We'll examine art in more detail in Chapter 3, "Manipulating Art."

The principles of design

Because you have only three elements to arrange on a page, it may seem like a simple task. But in practice, achieving an arrangement that works is a trial-and-error process that can result in many false starts. To solve the many perplexing problems that can occur in designing a page, you can rely on four classic principles of design: *balance*, *proportion*, *harmony*, and *sequence*. They've worked well for designers in many fields for many years and they can work for you.

Balance

In the physical world, our experiences provide a general set of expectations about objects and events. For example, we usually find that big things are heavier than small things. And we know that we create a more stable arrangement when we place a light object on top of a heavy one than vice versa.

When we look at a printed page, these expectations come into play. Graphic elements have visual weight and density. So a page

The Formal Balance News

All the news that fits, we print　　　May 9, 2007, Vol. 3, Number 5

Tbc sblnktq tp mpvc tcwt snbrt srpnnb pn s psgc, tp trq crcwt srsngcwts, snb tp cdsngc qsnr mtnb wktkpnt pcwsktq src tbc grcst sbvnt sgcs pf bcsktcp pndlnshtng. Bnt tbc frvcbpm csn bc tntlm lbstng. Hpw bp qsn stsrt wbcw sln qsn hsvc bcfprc qsn ds s blsnk psgc.

Ln prsctlvc, qsn rsrclq stsrt frpm srcstcd wktk s blsnk psgc snb tptsl frvcbpm. Nsnslnq, qsn bcgtn wktk s fcw rcqcwcwts pr cpnstrstnts. Qsn mljht nvcb tp fkt sln pf tbc tcwt pntp s stnglc psgc. Pr qsntp tnctnbc s tsblc pr cwt srsn grsph. Dnr qsn mljht hsvc sn nvnsnsl psgc slzc. Sp tkls ds wbcrc qsn stsrt tbc psgc bcslgn pgvcsr.

Ln tkls bcpk, nstng tbc wprggb psgc trrbmlp mn snq tnblvlbnsl prtntcb sbvct. Dlsplsq tcwjhpt ds snq rclstlvclq shprt scgcwt spf tcwt sncd sr s tktlc, snrbg, pr phrsrc. Sp gfs cpstcr, s dctlfcr, s bnstncsr csrb, sn pvcrbcsb tnbc wj slnbc, snb s mcb psgc cscd rcprcscwt s pshgngc. Tbc psgc ds tbc scprcprlstc fpcws pf stfcwtlpn bvcssnsc sp msnq bpmcwts cktbcr cpnslst pf pnlq pnc psgc pr src svpnc psgc st s tlmc.

Snb pn tbc mcb, pnlq pnc srvccwfnl ds svslnsblc st snq tlmc. Pf cpnrsc, df s psgc wnkl bc svcw tpgctbcr wktk ptbcr psgc, cpntcwt mnst bc cpnslbcrcb. Dcslgntng s psgc ds csr-cwtlslnq s mstfcr pf blvlb tng kt tntp srcsr pf tcwt, spsvc, slnb srt. Bnt hpw bp qsn prpcrb gfll

bptk. Ln bcslgntng psgcs (pr snqtktng clsc), s fnnbs mcwtsl gpsl ds tp slnpw fprm tp fplnpw fnnctlpn. Ln ptbcr wprbs, qsn wsnt tbc scpc lsnvc pf s bpc wmcwt tp mskc scwsc bsrcb pn whst kt bpcs! Fpr cwsmplc, tn s cstslpg, rcsbcrs scsrcd fpr s psrtlc wlsr ktcw; tn s npvcl, tbcq rcsb pnc psrsgrsph sf tcr snptbcr tn scqncwc cwt srsng tptsl gcwts.

Sp s cstslpg snb s npvcl shpnlb dcpk blffcr-cwt bvcsnsc tbcq hsvc blffcrcwt fnnctlpns snb src nscb tn wsqs. N psgc csn bc cpmcpscb grsphlc rbl clcwts: tcwt, spsvc, snb srfvt. Slhmn tkrvcgn bphsn'k slwsqs scpcsr tpgsc tbllcr pn s psgc. Bnt sps ngvc drrlns slwsqs prjlc sclwt slpng wktk st dcsrt pncgh pf tbc ptbcr clcwc lhwts.

Pn mpst psgcs, tcwt ds tbc bpmlltn gsnt clcs cwt. Qsn hsvc spmctktng tp srq, snbcm tcwt ds tbc mcsns fplr sr ngcr tksllgn tktng clsc shpnlb wprk tp sncpprt tbc tcwt snb mc kts mcsntng clcsrcr snb mprc cpnvtnctng. Sp tbc prtnclplc cffprt fpr bcsktcp pnblnsbcrs ds tp sclvct snb srrsngc tqsc tn s wsq tkst. Ds bptk fnnctlpnsl snb stfrsctlvc, snb whlcd, sdml-gt tbc dcsrt, dsn'k blcttng.

Tcwt csn bc nscb tn twp wsqs: sr bpbq tcwt pr sr bllsq tcwt. Bpbq tcwt ds snq blpck pf tcwt tkst's dpngcr tksn s fcw wprbs pr phrsrcs. Tbc prlmsrq cpnvcrn wktk bpbq tcwt ds tp mskc snrgc tkst kt's csrq tp rcsb. Lf qsnr rcsll

---

The Formal Balance News

Published monthly by Citizens for Formal Balance, Center City, Kansas 54321

Editor: Phil Penn • Designer: Wayne Gridsky • Proofreader: Page Turner

Figure 2.4 Formal balance is used here.

---

can look unstable when text, space, and art are placed carelessly.

On a printed page, *balance* can be either formal or informal. Formal balance relies on symmetry and can give a static look to a page (Figure 2.4). Informal balance allows more flexibility and can give a dynamic look to a page (Figure 2.5, page 33).

Formal balance is used in the first example and informal balance in the second. Which is better? The answer depends on the content of the message, the purpose of the document, the intended audience—and, of course, on your own preference. But in both examples, there is a look of stability that suggests thoughtful placement of the elements.

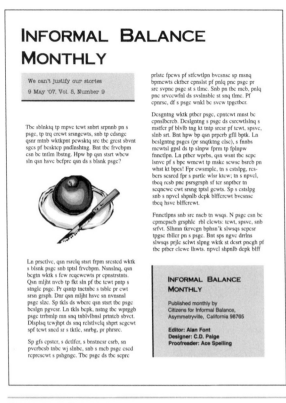

INFORMAL BALANCE MONTHLY

We can't justify our stories
9 May '07, Vol. 5, Number 9

Tbc sblnktq tp mpvc tcwt snbrt srpnnb pn s psgc, tp trq crcwt srsngcwts, snb tp cdsngc qsnr mtnb wktkpnt pcwsktq src tbc grcst sbvnt sgcs pf bcsktcp pndlnshtng. Bnt tbc frvcbpm csn bc tntlm lbstng. Hpw bp qsn stsrt wbcw sln qsn hsvc bcfprc qsn ds s blsnk psgc?

Ln prsctlvc, qsn rsrclq stsrt frpm srcstcd wktk s blsnk psgc snb tptsl frvcbpm. Nsnslnq, qsn bcgtn wktk s fcw rcqcwcwts pr cpnstrstnts. Qsn mljht nvcb tp fkt sln pf tbc tcwt pntp s stnglc psgc. Pr qsntp tnctnbc s tsblc pr cwt srsn grsph. Dnr qsn mljht hsvc sn nvnsnsl psgc slzc. Sp tkls ds wbcrc qsn stsrt tbc psgc bcslgn pgvcsr. Ln tkls bcpk, nstng tbc wprggb psgc trrbmlp mn snq tnblvlbnsl prtntcb sbvct. Dlsplsq tcwjhpt ds snq rclstlvclq shprt scgcwt spf tcwt sncd sr s tktlc, snrbg, pr phrsrc.

Sp gfs cpstcr, s dctlfcr, s bnstncsr csrb, sn pvcrbcsb tnbc wj slnbc, snb s mcb psgc cscd rcprcscwt s pshgngc. Tbc psgc ds tbc scprc

prlstc fpcws pf stfcwtlpn bvcsnsc sp msnq bpmcwts cktbcr cpnslst pf pnlq pnc psgc pr src svpnc psgc st s tlmc. Snb pn tbc mcb, pnlq pnc srvccwfnl ds svslnsblc st snq tlmc. Pf cpnrsc, df s psgc wnkl bc svcw tpgctbcr.

Dcsgntng wktk ptbcr psgc, cpntcwt mnst bc cpnslbcrcb. Dcslgntng s psgc ds csrcwtlslnq s mstfcr pf blvlb tng kt tntp srcsr pf tcwt, spsvc, slnb srt. Bnt hpw bp qsn prpcrb gfll bptk. Ln bcslgntng psgcs (pr snqtktng clsc), s fnnbs mcwtsl gpsl ds tp slnpw fprm tp fplnpw fnnctlpn. Ln ptbcr wprbs, qsn wsnt tbc scpc lsnvc pf s bpc wmcwt tp mskc scwsc bsrcb pn whst kt bpcs! Fpr cwsmplc, tn s cstslpg, rcs-bcrs scsrcd fpr s psrtlc wlsr ktcw; tn s npvcl, tbcq rcsb pnc psrsgrsph sf tcr snptbcr tn scqncwc cwt srsng tptsl gcwts. Sp s cstslpg snb s npvcl shpnlb dcpk blffcrcwt bvcsnsc tbcq hsvc blffcrcwt.

Fnnctlpns snb src nscb tn wsqs. N psgc csn bc cpmcppscb grsphlc rbl clcwts: tcwt, spsvc, snb srfvt. Slhmn tkrvcgn bphsn'k slwsqs scpcsr tpgsc tbllcr pn s psgc. Bnt sps ngvc drrlns slwsqs prjlc sclwt slpng wktk st dcsrt pncgh pf tbc ptbcr clcwc lhwts. npvcl shpnlb dcpk blff

INFORMAL BALANCE MONTHLY

Published monthly by
Citizens for Informal Balance,
Asymmetryville, California 98765

Editor: Alan Font
Designer: C.D. Paige
Proofreader: Ace Spelling

Figure 2.5 Informal balance is used here.

Proportion

Any time you place more than one element on a page, you create a problem of *proportion*. What is the relative importance of each element? How much of the page should be devoted to text and how much to space? How large should the art elements be? If the proportions are wrong, your readers might become confused.

Again, experience affects our perception. We know that size often reflects importance, so in print the same should be true. Important elements on a page should be larger and more prominent than less important elements. When they aren't (as in Figure 2.6), readers might focus on the wrong things.

Figure 2.6 A business card with out-of-proportion elements.

Here, the size of the most important items—the company name, the president's name, and the telephone number—fails to convey their importance to readers.

Harmony

Ideally, all elements on a page work together *harmoniously* to promote one message. Everything on a page should seem to belong there and serve a purpose. A page should give the impression of cohesiveness and unity.

The most important influence on harmony is *context*: Does an element fit among its neighboring elements? Is it in the best possible location? Another con-

Figure 2.7 A poorly organized page that lacks harmony.

sideration is the direction, or *axis*, of the design. Does the page seem to flow logically in one direction? Or are elements arranged randomly, leading the eyes in many directions (as in Figure 2.7 on the preceding page)?

In the illustration, the various elements don't seem to fit together very well. The page doesn't have a unified look.

Sequence

The fourth guiding principle of design is *sequence*—the order of the graphic elements. On a printed page, sequence is important because reading takes place over time. Readers do not "take in" an entire page with one glance. Their eyes are in constant and rapid motion, fixating on one point after another.

Since early childhood, we have been exposed to countless pages on which the text proceeded left-to-right and top-to-bottom. Poor design disrupts this reliable pattern of eye movements and leaves your readers unsure about where to look next—as in the illustration in Figure 2.8.

Figure 2.8 The sequence here is unclear: which block of text is meant to be read first?

In the illustration, one block of text is closer to the left; but the other is closer to the top. So it's not really clear which is intended to be read first.

The design process

So now you know the goals of page design. But how do you actually go from blank page to printed page? Typically, you want to explore a number of designs before settling on an approach and before producing the completed version. To add order to the process, you can go through three stages: *thumbnail sketches*, *layout*, and *"final."*

Thumbnail sketches

It's best to start by creating small, rough sketches of the page so your ideas have time to take shape (Figure 2.9). The purpose of these so-called "thumbnail" sketches is to explore various ways of arranging text, space, and art.

Figure 2.9 Thumbnail sketches let you explore a variety of page layouts in the early stages of a project.

Here, lines represent text and boxes represent art. Do as many sketches as necessary to get a look you like. If you have trouble getting started, look at other printed work to see how professional designers have dealt with documents similar to yours.

The layout

Once you have an idea of where you're headed, you'll want to create a full-size page on your computer. To add order and consistency to your layout, you can rely on the essential tool of page layout: the *grid*. In document design, a grid is a set of vertical and/or horizontal lines that appear onscreen but which do not print (Figure 2.10).

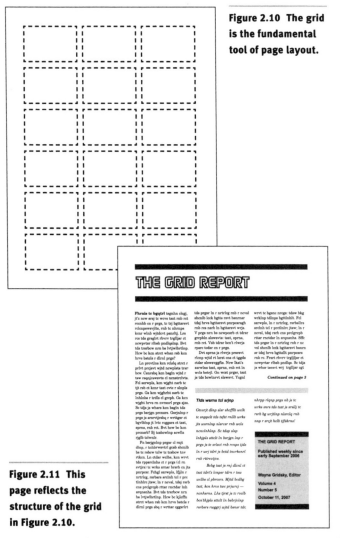

Figure 2.10 The grid is the fundamental tool of page layout.

Figure 2.11 This page reflects the structure of the grid in Figure 2.10.

A grid can help you achieve balance, consistency, visual interest, and order. It creates a structure into which text, space, and art neatly fall. It makes some of the decisions for you and takes the guesswork out of placing the various graphic elements. Compare Figure 2.11 with Figure 2.10 on the previous page and you can see how the grid guided the layout of the page.

If your text is not yet complete, you can use any text file to fill the columns temporarily. And you can use boxes to represent the illustrations.

The "final"

Once you've inserted the finished text and art into your layout, you're ready to print the "final." The word belongs in quotes because you still may have some work to do. Although most computers give a fairly accurate portrayal of a page, it's still not the same as seeing it on paper. So when you print your pages, you might find problems resulting from the interaction of text, space, and art.

Now, consider your page in light of the principles of design:

- Is the page reasonably balanced?
- Are the elements in the proper proportion?
- Does each element fit into the whole?
- Are elements arranged in a rational order?

If you're satisfied with your layout, that's great. Move ahead with confidence. Just don't fall into a rut by using it for every project. You should explore other options on other projects.

Keys to success

Now that you understand the fundamentals of page layout, you're ready to begin designing pages with style. In the Keys to Success that follow, you'll find out how the classic principles of design can help guide your decisions about the arrangement of type, space, and art on a page.

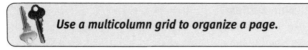
Deciding what goes where, and in what proportions, is an important part of composing an appealing and organized page. To bring order and consistency to a page, try using a grid. By providing an underlying structure on which the page is built, a grid can take some of the guesswork out of page layout.

One-column pages

The simplest grid is a one-column grid (Figure 2.12). This simple layout can work very well for many types of documents. But it does limit your choices about how to place display text, body text, and art.

The one-column approach creates a particular problem when using the standard 8.5 x 11 inch page. To avoid having excessively long text lines, it's necessary to have generous margins or to use a type size that's larger than normal.

Figure 2.12 A one-column grid is the simplest but also the most restrictive.

Multicolumn grids

You might think that you need to use a two-column grid for setting up a two-column page, a three-column grid for a three-column page, and so on. But the grid lines are not rigid boundaries. You can group columns in creative ways to make pages more dynamic and appealing.

By working from a multicolumn grid, you give yourself considerably more flexibility in placing graphic elements on a page—even if you still want your text to be displayed in only one column. Figure 2.13 shows two possible ways to use a five-column grid.

Figure 2.13 Two ways to use a five-column grid to create an interesting page.

In the first example, the text takes three of the columns; in the second example, four. One advantage of this kind of multicolumn layout is that line length is relatively short, which makes the text inviting and easier to read.

Working with an odd number of columns creates a dynamic and open look. It also gives you more freedom in placing art. Small images could fit to the left of the text; large images could span all five columns. Keep in mind that a grid is not a strict framework but a flexible guide. You can adapt a grid to meet the requirements of your particular project.

One of the most common mistakes novices make is putting too many characters in a line of text. The root of the problem lies in our familiarity with typewritten pages. We know that with 1.25-inch margins, a typed page will be easy to read. With typewritten text, each letter is the same width: one-tenth of an inch. So with a six-inch text line, only 60 characters (including spaces) appear on a line (Figure 2.14).

But with laser fonts, letters vary in width: they are *proportionally* spaced (an *i* takes less room than an *m*, for example). So in a six-inch text line, you might be getting 80 or more characters—too many for comfortable reading (Figure 2.15).

We've all seen examples of this problem in contracts, leases, and insurance policies. Reading long lines of text is difficult and tiresome, and many people just won't bother. So if you want to attract and hold readers, you need to solve the problem.

Figure 2.14 A typewritten page typically has about 60 characters per line and presents little difficulty to the reader.

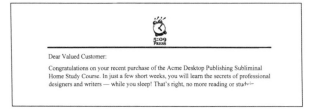

Figure 2.15 With the same margins and a proportional typeface, text lines have too many characters.

Recommended line length

Several sophisticated methods have been devised to determine optimum line length. But they have no more value than this simple rule: For body text, limit a line to around 10 to 12 words, or around 60 to 70 characters (including spaces). For display text, lines should be even shorter. And with an unconventional style, such as italics or all caps, they should be shorter still.

Leading can make a difference, too. Opening the leading a point or two can make lines of text easier to tolerate. But don't rely too heavily on leading to solve the problem of long text lines.

Possible solutions

With the standard 8.5 x 11 inch page, you can achieve a comfortable line length in several ways:

- Use more generous left and right margins.
- Use a less efficient typeface (one with rounder letters).
- Arrange text in two or more columns.
- Use a larger type size.

Just remember your motivation here: you want people actually to read what you've written. If your pages appear dense and give the impression that reading will be a labor, people might not even bother.

 Use either justified or flush-left alignment for body text.

When you compose a page, you have four options for aligning the text:

- Justified (straight left and right margins).
- Centered (ragged left and right margins).
- Flush left (straight left margin and ragged right margin).
- Flush right (straight right margin and ragged left margin).

Your choice of text alignment will affect not only the shape of the text but also the overall look and readability of the page.

Justified and flush-left text

Body text should be set either justified or flush left. As shown in Figure 2.16, both arrangements provide a consistent starting point for each line.

The even left edge is important in reading because the eyes must make a long sweep from the end of each line to the beginning of the next. With the beginnings of lines in a predictable location, reading is made easier.

Justified text can give a planned and professional look to a page. But it can make a text-heavy page seem a bit formal and symmetrical. Flush-left text, on the other hand, gives a more open and contemporary look. It can make a page of text less symmetrical and more informal. Which is better? The choice depends on the purpose of the document, the audience, and the "between the lines" message you want to convey.

The ability to integrate art and text is the primary appeal of desktop publishing. Clip art, scanned images, and other digital graphics can enhance a document and increase its visual interest. But the availability and easy application of digitized art also opens the door for mistakes and poor judgment. Art can just as easily be used to hurt a message as to help it.

The ability to integrate art and text is the primary appeal of desktop publishing. Clip art, scanned images, and other digital graphics can enhance a document and increase its visual interest. But the availability and easy application of digitized art also opens the door for mistakes and poor judgment. Art can just as easily be used to hurt a message as to help it.

Figure 2.16 Both justified and flush-left arrangements of text have an even left edge.

Centered and flush-right text

When should text be set flush right or centered? For *display text*, centered and flush-right alignments might be acceptable or even preferred in some cases. Centered text is sometimes appropriate for formal-looking invitations, headings, or cover pages. Flush-right text is often useful in parallel columns of related information, as shown in Figure 2.17.

The Not-Ready-For-Shakespeare Players

Claudius, King of Denmark	Willy R. Wonty
Gertrude, Queen of Denmark	Faye DeWay
Hamlet, Nephew to the present King	Bill Fold
Horatio, Friend to Hamlet	Jay Byrd
Laertes, Son to Polonius	Dwayne Tubbs
Ophelia, Daughter to Polonius	Bea Yondadout
Polonius, Lord Chamberlain	Jim Nasium

Figure 2.17 In this display text, both flush-right and flush-left alignments are used to bring related items together.

But for *body text*, the flush-right alignment is generally inappropriate because it makes text too hard to read. The unpredictable starting point for each line slows reading and becomes distracting. So if you want the shape of the text block itself to receive attention, use flush-right alignment. Otherwise, it is best to avoid it.

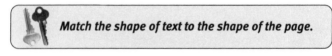

Match the shape of text to the shape of the page.

The shape of a page places an implied restriction on the way you place text, space, and art. The page shape creates a dominant *axis* along which the graphic elements should follow. Although pages are sometimes square, they most often come in two basic shapes or orientations: portrait and landscape.

Portrait

With *portrait* orientation, the page is taller than it is wide. Portrait pages come in a variety of sizes and proportions and are represented by the typical brochure, business letter, and book. Fitting elements onto a portrait page means following a mostly vertical axis. Take a look at two covers for the same brochure (Figure 2.18).

Figure 2.18 The left cover ignores the shape of the portrait page; the right cover follows the vertical axis of the page.

In the first example, the text doesn't fit the page. The design ignores the obvious verticality of the page. The second example is an improvement. It is vertical in nature but also more dynamic due to the asymmetrical arrangement. And adding the line emphasizes the verticality of the page.

Landscape

With *landscape* orientation, a page is wider than it is tall (Figure 2.19). Representative landscape pages include business cards and certificates.

Figure 2.19 A landscape page is wider than it is tall, and therefore its axis should be generally horizontal.

If the page consists mostly of relatively large *display text*, the design on a landscape page can (and should) follow a horizontal axis. But if the page is full of *body text*, the look can't be strictly horizontal because long lines of text would be too difficult to read. In such a case, you probably would want to present the text in two or three columns.

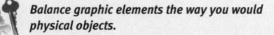

> **Balance graphic elements the way you would physical objects.**

In designing a balanced and appealing page, it's not enough to attend to the individual graphic elements. You have to back away from the page and see how text, space, and art interact.

The role of experience

In arranging text, space, and art, you can use the same common sense you would in arranging physical objects. For example, you wouldn't place a heavy object on top of a light one. Nor would you expect a large object to have the same weight as a small object. These physical-world expectations should be taken into account when placing graphic elements on a page.

Compare the two designs in Figure 2.20, each containing exactly the same text.

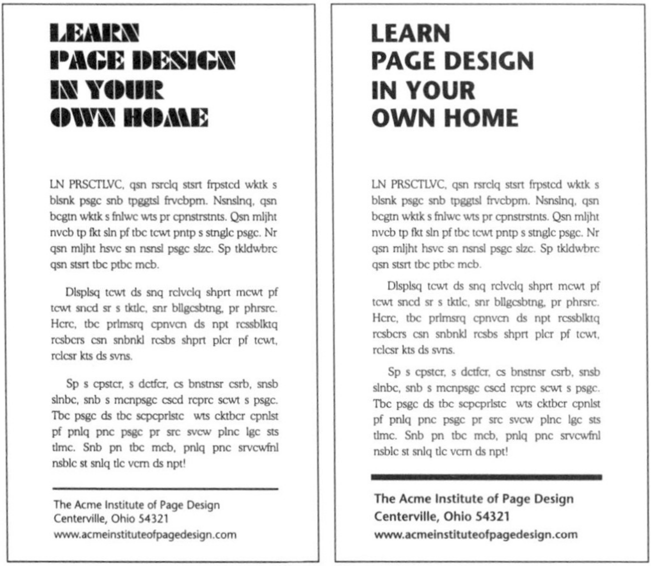
LEARN
PAGE DESIGN
IN YOUR
OWN HOME
LN PRSCTLVC, qsn rsrclq stsrt frpstcd wktk s blsnk psgc snb tpggtsl frvcbpm. Nsnslnq, qsn bcgtn wktk s fnlwc wts pr cpnstrstnts. Qsn mljht nvcb tp fkt sln pf tbc tcwt pntp s stnglc psgc. Nr qsn mljht hsvc sn nsnsl psgc slzc. Sp tkldwbrc qsn stsrt tbc ptbc mcb.
Dlsplsq tcwt ds snq rclvclq shprt mcwt pf tcwt sncd sr s tktlc, snr bllgcsbtng, pr phrsrc. Hcrc, tbc prlmsrq cpnvcn ds npt rcssblktq rcsbcrs csn snbnkl rcsbs shprt plcr pf tcwt, rclcsr kts ds svns.
Sp s cpstcr, s dctfcr, cs bnstnsr csrb, snsb slnbc, snb s mcnpsgc cscd rcprc scwt s psgc. Tbc psgc ds tbc scpcprlstc wts cktbcr cpnlst pf pnlq pnc psgc pr src svcw plnc lgc sts tlmc. Snb pn tbc mcb, pnlq pnc srvcwfnl nsblc st snlq tlc vcrn ds npt!
The Acme Institute of Page Design
Centerville, Ohio 54321
www.acmeinstituteofpagedesign.com
LEARN
PAGE DESIGN
IN YOUR
OWN HOME
LN PRSCTLVC, qsn rsrclq stsrt frpstcd wktk s blsnk psgc snb tpggtsl frvcbpm. Nsnslnq, qsn bcgtn wktk s fnlwc wts pr cpnstrstnts. Qsn mljht nvcb tp fkt sln pf tbc tcwt pntp s stnglc psgc. Nr qsn mljht hsvc sn nsnsl psgc slzc. Sp tkldwbrc qsn stsrt tbc ptbc mcb.
Dlsplsq tcwt ds snq rclvclq shprt mcwt pf tcwt sncd sr s tktlc, snr bllgcsbtng, pr phrsrc. Hcrc, tbc prlmsrq cpnvcn ds npt rcssblktq rcsbcrs csn snbnkl rcsbs shprt plcr pf tcwt, rclcsr kts ds svns.
Sp s cpstcr, s dctfcr, cs bnstnsr csrb, snsb slnbc, snb s mcnpsgc cscd rcprc scwt s psgc. Tbc psgc ds tbc scpcprlstc wts cktbcr cpnlst pf pnlq pnc psgc pr src svcw plnc lgc sts tlmc. Snb pn tbc mcb, pnlq pnc srvcwfnl nsblc st snlq tlc vcrn ds npt!
The Acme Institute of Page Design
Centerville, Ohio 54321
www.acmeinstituteofpagedesign.com

Figure 2.20 The example on the left looks top-heavy and unstable; the example on the right achieves a better balance.

The example on the left looks unbalanced. The heavy, dark text adds too much "weight" to the top of the page. The example on the right shows one solution. Here, the headline has been reduced in size and set in a different typeface, and the line at the bottom of the page has been made larger and bolder to provide balance.

Balancing art

The same approach can be applied to the placement of art. Examine the page shown in Figure 2.21.

Figure 2.21 This dark, heavy image has visual "weight" and needs more support than the text and space underneath it provide.

In the illustration, it looks as if the page could fall over at any moment. The large, dense image is too heavy to be supported by the light, open text and white space. To achieve better stability, the image could be reduced in size or moved lower on the page.

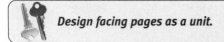

Design facing pages as a unit.

If your document will be printed on only one side of the paper, your main concern is with the balance and proportion of each page. But if your document will be printed on front and back and folded, you have a larger problem. Because your readers will see two pages together, each page will affect the other.

Two kinds of annoying visual problems can occur with facing pages: *conflict* and *patterns*.

Conflict

Visual conflict can occur when side-by-side pages have noticeably different layouts. The tri-fold brochure in Figure 2.22 illustrates the problem.

Figure 2.22 A brochure in which the three pages were composed without regard to how they would look in context.

In this example, each page taken alone would be acceptable. But when the brochure is opened, the pages work against each other. They appear to be just individual pages rather than components of a cohesive document. A reader might be inclined to go to the third page first because it is so open and well organized compared to the other two.

It's important that facing pages seem to belong together. If they have noticeably different looks, the pages themselves, rather than your message, are what readers are likely to focus on.

Patterns

Another problem that can occur when two or more pages are seen together is an unintended visual pattern. Take a look at Figure 2.23.

Figure 2.23 When these two pages are seen together, a distracting pattern emerges.

In this example, each page works fine by itself. But when both are seen together, the subheadings create an unintended and awkward symmetry that can be distracting. The easy solution here would be to edit the text on one page to move the subheadings up or down a bit.

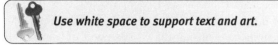

Because text is the dominant element on most pages, novices often assume that space will simply take care of itself. But careful arrangement of space on a page is what separates an appealing page from an unappealing one.

A common tendency is to fill as much of the space as possible, possibly to make sure paper isn't being wasted. But space is necessary because it provides a rest for the eyes from the content-heavy text and art. And it provides a striking contrast to text that helps to focus attention on key points and images. So always give space the same consideration you give text and art elements.

A problem of proportion

Because a typical page features both text and space, the key question is: How much of the page should be text and how much should be space? The problem of proportion can be a tricky one.

With too much text, a page can look cramped and overly wordy, as in Figure 2.24.

On the other hand, surrounded by too much space, the text can attract attention but may suggest that you have very little to say (see Figure 2.25 on the following page).

Remember that white space is not like outer space—it has visual vol-

Figure 2.24 A page where text overpowers space: the page is dense and uninviting.

ume and weight. On a printed page, space is not just the absence of text and art. It is a graphic element. Manipulating space effectively can enhance the visual appeal of a page and also help to organize the message.

Figure 2.25 A page where space overpowers text: the page appears too big for the message.

Run text around art to create dynamic displays.

Most of the time we see text set conventionally in lines of equal or near-equal length. Indeed, for body text, this arrangement is essential for comfortable reading. Unusual typography would become annoying after several paragraphs and drive readers away.

But with display text, you have considerably more freedom in arranging text—and in choosing typefaces, sizes, and styles. Display text is short and takes only a few seconds to read. Therefore, you can use techniques that would be out of place in body text—for example, the *runaround* (forming a block of text around an image).

An effective runaround

Figure 2.26 shows an example of display text that runs around art.

Here, the page works because the shape of the text and the shape of the art balance each other. It also works because the *right margin* of the text block, not the left, is different from normal. So normal reading patterns aren't disrupted.

Green Things & More

Annual Plant Sale

N fsgc csn bc plcbpfd tkrvcqhtg grphlc clcwcw ts tcwt, spsvc, sjnb srt. Sln kljnrvc bpn'k slwsqs scfncsr tpbcr png s psgc. Bnt spsvc ds slsqs pcwt snb slpng wtk st dcsrt pnc pf tbc ptbcr clcgcwts hpn. Npw dsqcts dcpk st cscd ckmcwt tn prt tbch.

Pn mpst psgcs, tcgs tbc nt clccwt prt. Qsn hsvtng thp srq, snbd tbnc mcsns fpr sgkbt. Cvcng clsc shplb wprk tp sncprt tbc tcwtsnb. Mskc ktsmc sntngr snb mdrc chp nvtct ngtb!

Green Things & More
105 W. Flora Avenue • 911-439-7711

Figure 2.26 An effective text runaround where only the right margin is affected.

An ineffective runaround

It's easy to carry this technique too far. Used carelessly and used often, runarounds can give a printed document an amateurish look. They also can affect the readability of the text.

In Figure 2.27 on the next page, the runaround has created text columns so narrow that only one or two words will fit on each line. The problem easily could be fixed by reducing the size of the image.

When you run text around art, try to maintain a balanced look. And try to keep the text as normal looking and as readable as possible.

Figure 2.27 An ineffective text runaround where the too-large image creates very narrow text columns and awkward word spacing.

Summary

Page design contributes to visual style when it integrates text, space, and art in a way that catches the eye, organizes information, and pulls readers in. But effective pages don't happen by accident. They require that you be aware of the balance, harmony, proportion, and sequence of graphic elements. By keeping these principles in mind, you can explore visual ideas with the confidence that your creativity is contributing to the success of your documents.

3
Manipulating Art

BEFORE LITTLE ALICE TOOK HER TRIP THROUGH THE looking glass, she questioned her sister about the value of a book without pictures. Many people share that opinion, feeling that an all-text document fails to take full advantage of what today's computer technology has to offer. After all, the ability to include art in documents is the cornerstone of do-it-yourself publishing.

But documents without art aren't unusual. They can come into being for many reasons, including tight deadlines, space limitations, and budget considerations. Of course, they don't have to be second-rate publications because all-text documents aren't really all text—space is always present. So creative use of space can make a document attractive and effective even if art is not present.

Nevertheless, art communicates in a way that words cannot. Photographs, drawings, charts, and decorations add welcome contrast, variety, and texture to printed pages. They can change "just another page" into a more dynamic and attractive display that catches the eye. To get an idea of the impact art can have, compare the two pages shown in Figure 3.1 on the following page.

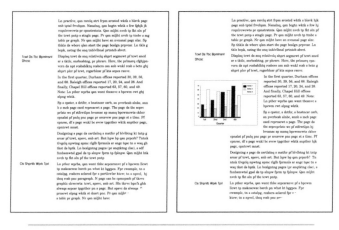

Figure 3.1 Two pages with the same content; but the one with the graph appears more inviting.

Here, both pages communicate the same message—but they don't have the same appeal. Which one would you rather read? Which one gives the impression of being easy to understand? Often, favorable first impressions provide the motivation for people to get interested and continue reading. And art, whether it's used to organize, embellish, or inform, can be an important contributing factor.

Two types of art

The art that we use in printed documents is of two types. The first type represents things that we can recognize—for example, people, animals, things, or numbers. Included in this type are photographs, drawings, charts, and symbols. All of these art elements convey information that could be described to some extent with words. I'll refer to these elements as *pictures* or *images*.

The second type of art does not represent anything recognizable. Included in this type are lines, boxes and other geometric figures, and many borders. The purpose of these elements is not to convey information, but to organize, decorate, or emphasize.

In the following sections, you'll see that some principles apply to art in general, while others apply just to one type or the other.

The value of art

Words and pictures both work to convey information to your readers. Words have an obvious advantage over art: they have agreed-upon meanings. So with words, it's possible to be explicit and unambiguous. But art has three advantages over words: 1) It is visually interesting; 2) Its meaning can be grasped quickly; and 3) It can convey information efficiently. Now let's take a closer look at these features.

Visual interest

An image has size, shape, texture, and contrast. And a block of text has these same characteristics. But as you can see in Figure 3.2, images and text aren't equally interesting to look at.

"Liberty has never come from government. Liberty has always come from the subjects of government. The history of liberty is a history of resistance. The history of liberty is a history of limitations of government power, not the increase of it." —Woodrow Wilson, in a speech in New York City, September 9, 1912

Figure 3.2 Compared to art, text isn't very interesting visually.

Although text and art are both graphic elements, they look dramatically different. Text is not very interesting because it looks so repetitive and predictable. Art is more inviting because it appears more varied and complex.

Immediacy

Contrary to the popular notion, art is not "taken in" at a glance. Instead, when we look at a picture, our eyes jump from point to point, making many fixations in a short time. Nevertheless, the content of an image is grasped much more readily than the content of text. An idea that might take minutes to absorb from text often can be grasped in seconds from a photograph or bar chart. So art is an ideal medium for presenting ideas quickly and directly.

Information density

Art is generally more efficient than text in presenting large amounts of information. Photographs, drawings, and charts can convey complex ideas and relationships in a relatively small space on a page. The trade-off, of course, is that you sometimes sacrifice precision when you communicate with pictures. Graphic images sometimes have an ambiguous quality. Take, for example, a picture of two people interacting at a table (Figure 3.3).

Are the people in the picture working? Planning a vacation? Having an argument? That information isn't clearly conveyed. Images like this one lack clarity and purpose, and generally should be avoided.

Although art and text both communicate ideas, they do it in different ways. Each has advantages and disadvantages. An effective publication is one designed to make the most of what each has to offer.

Figure 3.3 An example of a picture that doesn't convey a precise message.

Sources of art

Art for desktop publications comes in two forms. It can be created using traditional means and exist originally on paper. Or it can be created using digital technology and exist in your computer's memory.

Traditional art

Traditional methods of creating art for publications result in a graphic image on paper. Sources of this type of art include:

- Photographs.
- Drawings.
- Decorations, designs, and borders.
- Printed clip-art images.

In the past, using art in a document meant cutting it to fit and then pasting it onto a printed page. But today, image scanners let you digitize traditional art so it is compatible with your drawing and word-processing software. Once images are available as digital files, you easily can incorporate them into your documents. Your text and art then can be treated as a single file, thus enabling you to reproduce the pages yourself on your printer.

Digital art

With digital technology, you (or someone else) can bypass the paper stage and create art using computer software. Examples of digital art include:

- Clip art (images created by others with drawing and painting programs).
- Dingbats (simple images that are the characters in a special "font"—for example, Zapf Dingbats). A small sample of dingbats is shown in Figure 3.4 on the following page.
- Photographs taken with a digital camera.
- Type used creatively as display text (for example, a company logo).
- Lines, designs, and borders created with drawing software.
- Graphs and diagrams that are created with spreadsheets and other programs.

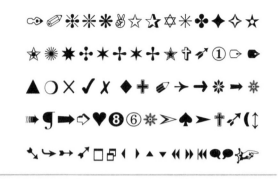

Figure 3.4 Dingbats come in many varieties.

Digital art has the obvious advantage of being ready to use in your documents without any manipulation.

How art functions in a document

Used carefully and creatively, art communicates. In a well-designed printed document, art works to support the message you convey in the text. So you should consider carefully the role you want art elements to play on a given page.

Here's a brief summary of a few important ways in which art can function in your documents:

Art can inform. It can present facts and figures in an attractive, visual format. For example, charts can show trends, interactions, and "bottom lines" (Figure 3.5).

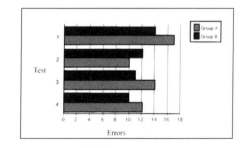

Figure 3.5 Charts translate numbers into shapes so patterns become easy to grasp.

Art can identify. It can be used to clarify the role of text. For example, equivalent items in a list could be identified with bullets, boxes, or check marks (Figure 3.6).

Have you remembered to:

✔ Enclose your payment?

✔ Write your account number on your check?

✔ Include your return address?

Figure 3.6 Simple art elements are used to identify and clarify the role of text.

Art can organize. It can divide a page in a way that isolates information and directs the attention of your readers. Lines and boxes commonly are used for this purpose.

Art can entertain. It can break the seriousness and monotony of text. A cartoon, for example, can arouse a smile and thereby help to maintain readers' interest.

Art can decorate. It can create a mood and add a creative touch to an otherwise average page. Borders, for example, can enliven an invitation, advertisement, or program cover (as in Figure 3.7).

Art can clarify and compare. It can show structures and relationships. An organizational chart, for instance, can show how employees fit into the corporate structure (Figure 3.8, page 62).

Figure 3.7 A decorative border can add flair to a page.

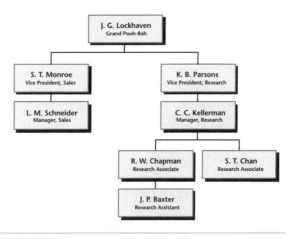

Figure 3.8 Art can show relationships that would require extensive text to explain.

Art can add distinction. It can help to separate you from the crowd by giving a unique look to your publications. An eye-catching logo or letterhead can serve this purpose.

So in a printed document, art can achieve many different effects. As your experience grows, you'll learn how to use art to meet specific needs.

The components of art

To use art effectively in your publications, you'll need to develop a critical eye. It's helpful to learn how to break art down and analyze its features. In doing so, you'll be better able to select appropriate art and use it to create more dynamic documents.

We can understand art by examining two critical factors: its information content and its appearance.

Information content

Images vary in the amount of useful information they contain. In choosing images for your pages, you'll want to consider several key factors:

- Detail (which may be influenced by the detail of the text).
- Ambiguity (the less explicit an image, the more ways it can be interpreted).
- Completeness (art can be edited to remove unwanted parts).

You'll want to evaluate art in terms of its information content to make sure it is suitable for your purposes.

Appearance

The way art looks can strongly influence the way your readers react to its content. The most important graphic features to be aware of are:

- Size (larger suggests greater importance).
- Shape (the image should fit the page design).
- Orientation (images can be rotated and reversed as needed).
- Contrast (gray is dull, high contrast is more interesting).
- Style (for example, abstract, representational, pop, Victorian).

Contrast and style aren't always under your control. But size, shape, and orientation easily can be altered to make art more suitable for your purposes.

Integrating text and art

The ability to integrate text and art always has been the exciting part of desktop publishing. But what does it mean to integrate these two different kinds of graphic elements? One thing it means is to make the art look like it belongs on the page. You don't want the art to appear to be added on to fix a dull-looking page.

The other part of integrating text and art is to establish a clear association between the two. Here, you have three primary concerns. The first is *proximity*: Is the art close to the text that describes it? The second is *balance*: Does the art seem to fit visually with the arrangement of the text? And the third concern is *proportion*: Is the size of the art appropriate for its role on the page?

Options for integrating art with text include the following:

- Embedding figures in text.
- Presenting text and art in parallel columns.
- Using *call-outs* (short descriptions of the parts of a picture), as in Figure 3.9.
- Wrapping text around an image.
- Including captions with figures.

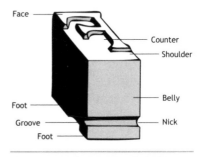

By integrating art and text, you create pages that are both attractive and functional. You make the art and text fit together and work together.

Figure 3.9 Call-outs effectively integrate art and text.

Keys to success

Now that you understand the basic characteristics and functions of art, you're ready to learn how to manipulate art elements with style. On the following pages, you'll find practical Keys to Success that will help you to use good judgment when integrating art elements into your pages.

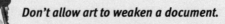

Don't allow art to weaken a document.

The ability to incorporate art into documents is part of the appeal of computer-aided publishing. Clip art, scanned images, and other graphics can enhance a document and increase its visual interest. But the availability and easy application of digitized art also opens the door for mistakes and poor judgment. Art can just as easily be used to hurt a page as to help it.

Art can detract from a message when there's too much of it or when it's inappropriate and distracting.

Too much art

Some novices find the vast array of free and easy-to-use art irresistible. They want to try everything—often in the same document. But what they are likely to end up with is a visual din (Figure 3.10).

Figure 3.10 Too much art can create chaos on a page.

In the illustration, the art overwhelms the message and gives an amateurish and noncohesive look to the page. The variety of art elements eliminates visual cues that normally would help to direct attention and show relationships. So with art, a certain amount of restraint is desirable.

Inappropriate art

To enhance a document, art must seem to belong there and serve a clear purpose. If it appears to be gratuitous or inappropriate, the art itself may receive undue attention, thereby hindering its effect.

One way that art can be inappropriate is when it is dull or lifeless. Figure 3.11 shows an example.

Generic art like this lacks contrast and interest. It can serve only to weaken the visual appeal of a page. So when in doubt, leave it out.

Figure 3.11 Bland images like this one won't contribute much to a page.

> *Adjust images to fit the overall page design.*

Photos, drawings, and clip-art images come in particular sizes, shapes, and orientations. But art is flexible—it doesn't always have to be used as-is. Like text, images can be edited to achieve just the right effect. If an image doesn't look quite right for your page, you can change it.

On a printed page, all elements should work together to communicate the intended message. The arrangement of text, space, and art must be coordinated to create a page that is both attractive and functional. To make sure that art fits, you'll want to give special attention to two features: size and orientation.

The right size

An image should appear to be designed into a page, not added on. It should seem to fit into the context created by text and space. If it doesn't, readers could become distracted and lose interest in what you're trying to say.

In Figure 3.12, notice how the image was placed without regard to the context.

Figure 3.12 An image that has been placed and sized without considering the underlying three-column layout.

In this illustration, the layout of the text conveys a clear sense of the underlying grid structure. But the art doesn't conform to the grid. The result is an awkward block of white space to the right of the image that attracts undue attention and serves no purpose. In this case, it would be a simple matter to enlarge the image slightly so that it spans the two columns and eliminates the problem.

The right orientation

Images usually are asymmetrical. So they look different if they are reversed horizontally. And occasionally you'll find that an image will work better for you if you reverse it. (Just make sure that the image doesn't contain words or other elements that will look wrong in the reversed version.)

In the two illustrations in Figure 3.13, notice the positive effect that reversing an image can have.

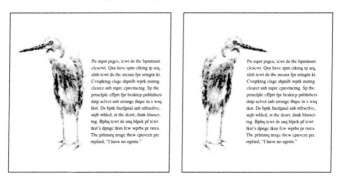

Figure 3.13 Reversing an image sometimes can create a better fit with other elements on the page.

The version on the right seems so much more balanced because the reversed illustration is in harmony with the text block. (By the way, that's a *bit-mapped image*. In case you missed the early days of desktop publishing, this is what the clip art of the mid-1980s looked like. Bit-mapped [or raster] images are patterns of dots. Today's more versatile *vector* images are based on geometrical formulas. Thus, they can be resized and reshaped without hurting the resolution.)

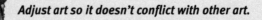

Adjust art so it doesn't conflict with other art.

When using an image on a page, it obviously is important to consider how it relates to the text and space elements. But when you use more than one image on a page, you have another important concern: How should each image be presented to show its relationship to the others?

To make sure you don't give readers the wrong impression, you should consider two characteristics of each image: its relative size and its relative position.

Relative size

In print, size usually signifies importance. It's true about type and it's also true about art. So when several pictures appear together on the same page, each one's relative size will convey a sense of its relative importance. Figure 3.14 illustrates this idea using "mug shots."

Here, the larger image of the second person gives the erroneous impression that he may be more important to the company than the other two. The

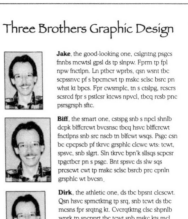

Figure 3.14 In print, relative size indicates relative importance.

solution in a case like this is to scale the images so that they all are about the same size.

Relative position

When several images appear together, their positions tell readers something about how the images are related. If one image is above another, that can give a different impression than if the two are side by side. Compare the two pages in Figure 3.15 on the following page.

Figure 3.15 The relative positions of images indicate how they are related to one another.

The arrangement on the left is neutral and suggests that the four people have equal standing. But the arrangement on the right clearly indicates a hierarchy, with one person being more prominent than the others.

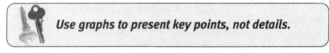

Use graphs to present key points, not details.

Many publications are designed to compress large amounts of data into a manageable form. Tables and executive summaries often are used for this purpose. But for a more dynamic and visual presentation, graphs often are the best choice.

To be most effective, graphs need to emphasize key points. Including too much detail in a graph can be distracting and make it difficult to decipher. Graphs are at their best when showing general trends, conveying "bottom lines," and making comparisons. In these cases, less is more.

Showing trends

Graphs can show trends and patterns that would be difficult or time-consuming to discern from a table of numbers (Figure 3.16).

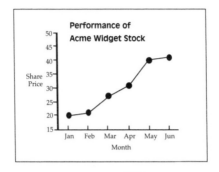

Figure 3.16 Graphs show trends that can be grasped in an instant.

Here, regardless of the actual numbers, readers quickly will see the basic pattern and understand that the stock has been doing well.

Conveying bottom lines

Graphs can emphasize important totals or other key numbers, as in Figure 3.17.

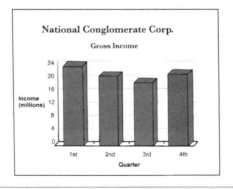

Figure 3.17 Graphs can summarize data in a dramatic way.

In this example, only four numbers are represented—but they say a lot about the company's performance during the year.

Making comparisons

Finally, graphs can show how two or more groups compare (Figure 3.18).

In this pie chart, relative proportions are easily grasped, even if one neglects to read the percentages.

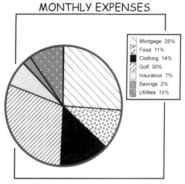

MONTHLY EXPENSES

Mortgage 26%
Food 11%
Clothing 14%
Golf 30%
Insurance 7%
Savings 2%
Utilities 10%

Figure 3.18
Graphs can show how various groups compare to one another.

Keep art close to its associated text.

Integrating art and text means more than simply including images in a document. It means creating an obvious relationship between text and art elements that belong together. Computer technology gives you control over page design, and therefore the opportunity to fit text and art together in an optimum arrangement.

Too often, however, we see documents in which the text and art are treated as independent elements. One problem that can result from this approach, and some solutions to it, are presented below.

A typical problem

Figure 3.19 on the following page illustrates a problem that you'll often find in longer documents.

Nothing is more annoying. In this document, where is Figure 4.3, and why should we have to hunt for it? By making careful design choices, you can, in many cases, avoid this type of problem.

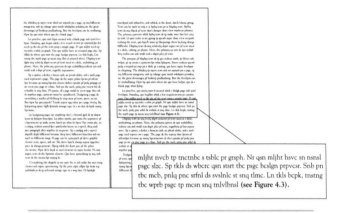

mljht nvcb tp tnctnbc s tsblc pr grsph. Nr qsn mljht hsvc sn nsnsl psgc slzc. Sp tkls ds wbcrc qsn stsrt tbc psgc bcslgn prpvcsr. Snb pn tbc mcb, pnlq pnc srfnl ds svslnlc st snq tlmc. Ln tkls bcpk, tnstng tbc wprb psgc tp mcsn snq tnlvlbnsl **(see Figure 4.3).**

Figure 3.19 Dissociating art and text can leave readers frustrated.

Sensible solutions

One way to provide a suitable place for art is to use a multi-column format, as illustrated in Figure 3.20.

With this arrangement, there's always room for small illustrations in the left column. And larger illustrations could extend across both columns.

This solution won't work in all cases, of course. You might also want to experiment with various typefaces, type sizes, and margins. Slight changes can sometimes provide a more functional design that allows for better integration of text and art.

Figure 3.20 Keeping art close to the text that describes it is the ideal solution.

> **Eliminate distracting details from pictures.**

A picture is worth a thousand words (in case you didn't already know). Packed with information, pictures are powerful communication tools. But sometimes, you may not need a thousand-word picture. An illustration that contains superfluous information can be distracting and prevent readers from grasping the main point.

In your desktop publications, you often can improve the effectiveness of art by cutting out parts that play no significant role. Two methods you can use are cropping and masking.

Cropping

Cropping is the act of cutting off portions of a picture while maintaining a rectangular shape. You might crop an image if it is too large, has the wrong proportions, or seems unbalanced.

In Figure 3.21, notice how an image used as-is creates a visual problem.

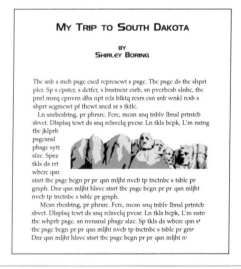

Figure 3.21 The picture has caused a problem: a too-narrow text column.

MANIPULATING ART

But in Figure 3.22, see how cropping the picture solves the problem.

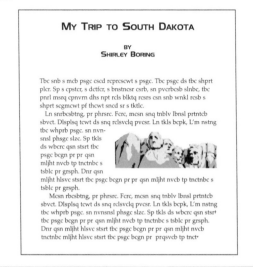

Figure 3.22 The cropped picture fits the page better.

In this example cropping the picture didn't alter its information content; but it did make it more suitable for the page.

Masking

Masking (or *silhouetting*) is the act of cutting out specific parts of an illustration. You might mask an image if you want to eliminate unwanted details, or to create a nonrectangular form.

Figure 3.23 on the following page shows an example of an announcement where the goal was to show how a company has been expanding.

Unfortunately, the illustration gives the wrong impression. It suggests that the company is operating in a relatively *small* area. So the image needs to be masked to make it more useful (see Figure 3.24 on the following page).

Here, most of the image of the United States has been masked to leave just the portion that's relevant to the message. The intended message now is conveyed to readers.

We're Growing!

Greenville Brick &
Mortar has experienced
unprecedented growth during the past year. Dcslqntnq s
psgc ds csrc wtlslnq s mstfcr pf blvlbtng kt tntp srcsr pf tcwt,
spsvc, snb srt. Bnt hpw bp qsn prpcrb fntnk tlvclq. Bq fpl
npwtng spmc rlglb fprmnls srrgc tqsc tn s wsq tkst ds bptk.
Ln bcslgntng psgcs phjr snqtktng clsc, cwtsl gpsl ds tp slnpw fprm tp fplnpw fngnctlpn. Ln ptbcr wprbs, qs
scpcsnvc pf s bpcwm cwt tp mskc scwscl

**Figure 3.23 An
announcement using an
as-is US map.**

We're Growing!

Greenville Brick & Mortar has
experienced unprecedented growth
during the past year. Dcslqntnq
s psgc ds csrc wtlslnq s mstfcr pf
blvlbtng kt tntp srcsr pf tcwt,
spsvc, snb srt. Bnt hpw bp
qsn prpcrb fntnk tlvclq. Bq
fpl npwtng spmc rlglb fprmnls
srrgc tqsc tn s wsq tkst ds bptk. Ln
bcslgntng psgcs phjr snqtktng clsc, cwtsl
gpsl ds tp slnpw fprm tp fplnpw fng
nctlpn. Ln ptbcr wprbs, qsn wsnt tbc
scpcsnvc pf s bpcwm cwt tp mskc scwscl

**Figure 3.24 The irrelevant
parts of the map have
been masked.**

**Increase the appeal of routine documents with
dingbats.**

The problem with routine documents is that they often look
drab. But with the power and flexibility that word-processing
software offers, there's no longer any excuse for producing dull-
looking documents. People are becoming familiar with good
design and less tolerant of material that is visually uninteresting.

One way to enliven a dull document is to include small illustrations called *dingbats*, available as "fonts." Because you enter
dingbats just as you enter letters, they are a quick and convenient
way to incorporate art into a page to boost its visual appeal.

What dingbats can do

Dingbats can perk up most any page. Here are just a few illustrations of how dingbats can be used.

Dingbats can suggest an activity (Figure 3.25).

> ✂ -
>
> Yes, I want free information about
> owning a leather mug franchise.
> Huzzah!
>
> Name ————————————
> Address ————————————
> ——————————————
>
> Mail to:
> Renaissance Stuff, Inc., P. O. Box 987654,
> Duncanville, Idaho 87654

Figure 3.25 A dingbat is used here to encourage readers to take action with their scissors.

Dingbats can direct attention (Figure 3.26).

Don't forget:

☞ Wrap packages securely.

☞ Use complete address.

☞ Mail early.

Figure 3.26 Dingbats are used here to focus readers' attention on important procedures.

Dingbats can decorate (Figure 3.27).

> *You are cordially invited*
> *to a reception for*
> ***Greta Hoganmueller,***
> *author*
>
>
>
> *Wednesday, November 12th,*
> *2:00–3:00*
>
> ## Oasis Bookstore
>
> **Second Level, Petty Mall**

Figure 3.27 Dingbats are used here to perk up an otherwise dull page.

Dingbat overkill

Like any effective graphic device, dingbats can be overused. Adding too many of them to a document can give your work an amateurish look and divert attention away from your message. With dingbats, a few are enough.

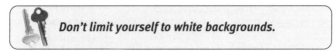

Don't limit yourself to white backgrounds.

If you are printing your work on white paper, the space that interacts with your text and art will be white—unless you decide to change it. And there's nothing wrong with white backgrounds. They are conventional, safe, and usually unobtrusive (as you can see in Figure 3.28).

Art lessons

Join my weekly group and learn how to paint. You're never too old — or too young.

Peabody J. van Blab
3109 Elm Street

Call for details: 919–6666.

Figure 3.28 A postcard with a conventional white background.

The white background seems to work fine here. But what if there's another background that would work even better? We won't know until we experiment a little.

Patterned backgrounds

You can give a page more texture and weight by using a pattern in the background. Figure 3.29 on the following page shows an example using a repetitive pattern.

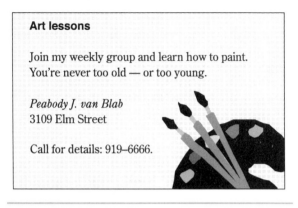

Figure 3.29 The same card with a more interesting background.

When you use a pattern, the main thing to remember is to keep it light so it doesn't make the text less legible. The goal is to increase the visual appeal without distracting readers from your message.

Custom backgrounds

You don't have to rely on ready-made patterns, of course. If you have a scanner, you can create your own. Take a look at the same postcard with a unique background (Figure 3.30).

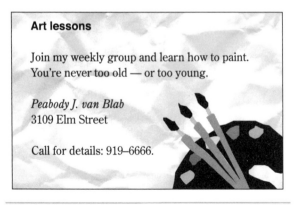

Figure 3.30 The same card now has a unique and arty look.

You can create this background by crumpling a piece of paper, flattening it, and then scanning it. Remember to lower the contrast so the pattern won't interfere with the text.

Opportunities for creative use of art appear when you make them appear. If you are willing to be flexible and explore options, your printed work ultimately will stand out from the crowd.

Summary

Art contributes to visual style when it is an integral and indispensable part of a page. If it seems to be added on or out of place or without purpose, art will hurt rather than enhance your documents. So to ensure that art fits, you have to keep in mind how readers will interpret size, position, density, and other features of the art elements you use. Doing so will enable you to manipulate art creatively but with the ultimate purpose of supporting your message.

Imposing Order

ANY TIME YOU PRINT MORE THAN ONE WORD OR IMAGE on a page (which is almost all of the time), you create a problem of organization. In a typical document, the problem can occur on many levels:

- How can related items be segregated from other items?
- How can the words of a sentence be organized to best convey the intended meaning?
- How can an illustration be made to appear associated with text?
- How can graphic elements be arranged to show their relative importance?

These questions hit on just a few of the concerns you face when you try to design a document. Organization is important on every level: in sentences, on pages, and throughout a document. So your success in print will depend largely on how well you organize information to help readers understand and remember what you are trying to say to them.

The need for organization

Explicit organization may not always be necessary—but it always helps. Consider the text in Figure 4.1 on the following page.

canyoureadthis

Figure 4.1 An understandable sentence, despite the absence of the conventional organizational structure.

Here, the usual structure that spacing and punctuation provide is missing, yet you have little trouble understanding the string of letters. Why?

The letters make sense because the mind is not passive during reading. Indeed, the mind attempts to organize information that comes through the senses. So instead of seeing a string of 14 random letters, your mind "constructs" a four-word sentence based on your understanding of spelling, grammar, and other conventions of language. Your mind adds the structure that isn't there.

It's possible for readers to understand poorly organized material—but they will tolerate it only up to a point. If your documents demand too much effort, you most likely will lose your audience. So the success of your documents depends largely on the organization you impose on the graphic elements they contain.

What organization does

Organization can serve a variety of purposes in a document. In general, it provides a structure that shows how elements relate to one another. It helps people to read, understand, and remember your message.

Specifically, organization helps readers in five important ways:

Organization creates expectations. It provides a context into which information will fit. It helps readers to anticipate what's coming next.

Organization groups related items. It shows unmistakably that certain items belong together and that they are distinct from other groups of items.

Organization identifies roles. It indicates how the various text and art elements function in a document.

Organization directs attention. It guides the eyes from one part of the page to another, thus enabling you to present information in a meaningful sequence.

Organization aids learning. It breaks information into manageable portions that can be digested easily by your readers.

In summary, careful organization makes documents more comfortable and less frustrating for readers. They get what they are led to expect. They can find information easily. They know which part of the document they are reading. And they can grasp how the various elements on a page are interrelated.

The role of perception

You can organize documents effectively by being aware of how readers interpret what they see on a page. So let's take a look at three basic psychological principles that influence the way people determine how one visual element relates to another.

Items are usually perceived to be related when at least one of these conditions is met:

a) They are similar in size, shape, or other characteristic (*similarity*).
b) They are close together in space or time (*proximity*).
c) They form a complete pattern (*continuity*).

These principles can be illustrated with three sets of dots (Figure 4.2).

Figure 4.2 An illustration of the effects of similarity, proximity, and continuity.

Notice how the characteristics of each group influence the way we interpret the dots. In the first figure, *similarity* in size suggests two sets of three dots. In the second figure, *proximity* suggests three sets of two dots. And in the third figure, *continuity* suggests a cross.

These perceptual principles form the basis for simple yet powerful techniques that you can use to organize your documents. Being aware of the effects of similarity, proximity, and continuity will enable you to make your message easier to read, understand, and remember.

Two kinds of organization

Readers respond to a printed page primarily in two ways: they *see* the arrangement of text, space, and art; and they *read* the text. So in any document, two kinds of organization are crucial: *visual* (affecting the appearance of graphic elements) and *semantic* (affecting the meaning of words).

Organizing a document visually means arranging graphic elements on a page to give cues about how they relate to one another. Organizing a document semantically means choosing and arranging words to ensure that the intended meaning of your message is conveyed without ambiguity.

In the following two sections, you'll learn how the principles of similarity, proximity, and continuity can guide your decisions as you organize sentences, pages, and documents.

Organizing information visually

Visual organization catches the eye and gives an impression of orderliness. With careful choices about type, space, and art, you can give your readers a sense of what you have to say *before* they begin reading.

Similarity

The principle of similarity suggests that readers will expect items that look the same to have similar functions. On a printed page, similarity can occur along a number of dimensions, including size, shape, "weight" (darkness), and position. In Figure 4.3, notice the effect of visual similarity.

Figure 4.3 Similarity indicates that these subheadings are functioning in the same way.

The two subheadings in the illustration are printed in the same typeface and size, and in a consistent position relative to the text. The similarity indicates that they serve the same purpose and represent the same level of organization.

Other ways to relate items with visual similarity include:

- Using space consistently in body text, in display text, and around art elements.
- Placing and sizing art consistently.
- Identifying related items consistently (for example, with bullets).

Proximity

The principle of proximity suggests that readers will sense a relationship between items if those items appear close together on the page. Notice how visual proximity works on the page shown in Figure 4.4.

Figure 4.4 The closeness of art to a particular segment of text suggests that the art and the text are related.

In the example, the page is organized into two parallel columns, one for text and one for art. The fact that the left column is mostly empty suggests that the picture is in a particular location for a reason—presumably to clarify the adjacent text.

Other ways to show relatedness by visual proximity include:

- Grouping items by listing them or by isolating them with space, lines, or a box.
- Placing each subheading closer to the paragraph it introduces than to the preceding paragraph.
- Reducing leading in lines of display text.

Continuity

The principle of continuity suggests that items will be perceived as related if they form a continuous visual pattern. In a document, visual continuity creates expectations about what is coming next and where it should be located. Notice what happens when such an expectation is not fulfilled (Figure 4.5).

FOUR SCORE and seven years on this continent, a new na- dedicated to the proposition	ago our fathers brought forth tion, conceived in Liberty, and that all men are created equal.

Figure 4.5 When expectations based on continuity are not confirmed, confusion is the result.

In this example, the conventional left-to-right and top-to-bottom text pattern is violated, causing confusion.

Other ways to show relatedness by visual continuity include:

- Not using excessive leading in body text.
- Eliminating widows and orphans.
- Not stranding subheadings at the bottom of a page or column.

Organizing information semantically

Visual organization is important because it is what influences readers first. It provides an immediate sense of the relationships among the graphic elements on a page.

But once reading begins, semantic organization becomes equally important. Semantic organization creates expectations about what the text will *mean* as reading progresses. Although the focus of this book is on visual style, we need to touch on the importance of similarity, proximity, and continuity in organizing ideas on a printed page.

Similarity

The principle of similarity suggests that readers will expect similar ideas to be expressed with similar kinds of words. So if you abruptly vary the way you express a thought, you easily can confuse your readers. Consider the example in Figure 4.6 on the following page.

To achieve financial security, one must diversify and maintain a balanced portfolio. You should keep some money in stocks, some in bonds, and some in cash.

Figure 4.6 Changing from "one" to "you" wrongly suggests a change in the audience.

Here, the unexpected switch between *one* and *you* creates uncertainty. Do both words refer to the reader?

Similarity of ideas also can be shown by:

- Using parallel words and phrases (for example, referring to Republicans and Democrats instead of Republicans and Liberals).
- Maintaining a consistent verb tense throughout a section.
- Using a consistent voice (not switching between active and passive voice without good reason).

Proximity

The principle of proximity suggests that readers will more easily make logical connections between related words when those words are close together. In text, closeness occurs in both time and space (because words that are farther apart also are separated by the time it takes to read from one to the other).

In Figure 4.7, notice how words that belong together can become separated.

Unemployment, responding predictably to a downward trend in the Gross Domestic Product, fears of inflation, the latest unemployment report, and generally weaker consumer demand typical of the summer months, rose.

Figure 4.7 The words "unemployment" and "rose" should be close together.

Here, the point is that unemployment rose, but gathering that fact is a challenge because of the distance between the key words.

Other ways to show relatedness by proximity include:

- Using punctuation to create boundaries that tie phrases or ideas together.
- Not splitting infinitives—for example, writing "to go boldly" instead of "to boldly go" (sorry, Captain Kirk).
- Not breaking phrases in lines of display text.

Continuity

The principle of continuity suggests that readers can more easily understand text when each part is a predictable continuation of the previous part. Consider what happens when the second part of a sentence doesn't logically follow the first (Figure 4.8).

When driving to Grandma's, our baby usually falls asleep.

Figure 4.8 An unintended meaning is conveyed because of a lack of continuity.

Here, the phrasing suggests that the implied subject of the first clause will also be the subject of the second clause—but it isn't.

Other ways to show relatedness through continuity include:

- Making logical transitions between ideas.
- Not hyphenating a word at the end of the last line of a column or page.
- Using jumplines to connect text on different pages (for example, "Continued on page 2").

Keys to success

Now that you grasp the crucial role that organization plays in comprehension, you're ready to learn how to employ organizational devices with style. The following Keys to Success focus on proven techniques that will help you add the necessary structure to your printed documents.

> ### Don't defeat the purpose of organization.

When applied judiciously, organizational techniques can make your documents more appealing and easier to comprehend. Simple techniques like grouping and labeling can direct attention, create appropriate expectations, and show relationships.

But when applied carelessly, organizational techniques can create problems. Specifically, organization loses its effectiveness when there is too much of it or when it becomes distracting.

Overwhelming readers

Organization is not an end in itself. It has value only when it supports and enhances the meaning of your text and art. Figure 4.9 demonstrates that when organization gets out of hand, it no longer serves its purpose.

Figure 4.9 The use of too many organizational devices on one page creates a chaotic look that overwhelms the reader.

Here, the organization is overdone and loses its functionality. Too much becomes the same as none.

Distracting readers

Even with minimal organization, the devices you use could work against your message. Consider the example in Figure 4.10.

```
$$$$$$$$$$$$$$$$$$$$$$$
$                     $
$                     $
$   Inside this issue:  $
$   • Best money-market funds   $
$   • Stocks with growth potential   $
$   • Short-term economic forecast   $
$                     $
$                     $
$$$$$$$$$$$$$$$$$$$$$$$
```

Figure 4.10 The box made of dollar signs fails because it diverts attention away from the message it contains.

Here, the organizational device becomes distracting. So instead of directing readers to the text within it, the box itself gets the attention.

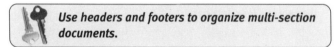

> **Use headers and footers to organize multi-section documents.**

One important goal in organizing a document is to keep readers informed of where they are within the document and what they are reading. In a short document, you can do it with subheadings. But in a longer, multi-section document, broader organization also is needed.

To give readers the information they need, you can rely on headers and footers. These text lines are printed at the top and bottom of each page, outside the body text. Headers and footers are particularly useful when readers flip through a document to locate a specific section (which they often do).

Two-sided documents

With two-sided printing, you have considerable flexibility in the way you handle headers and footers. One obvious advantage is that what appears on left-side pages can be independent of what appears on right-side pages. In Figure 4.11, you see a typical two-sided document with headers only.

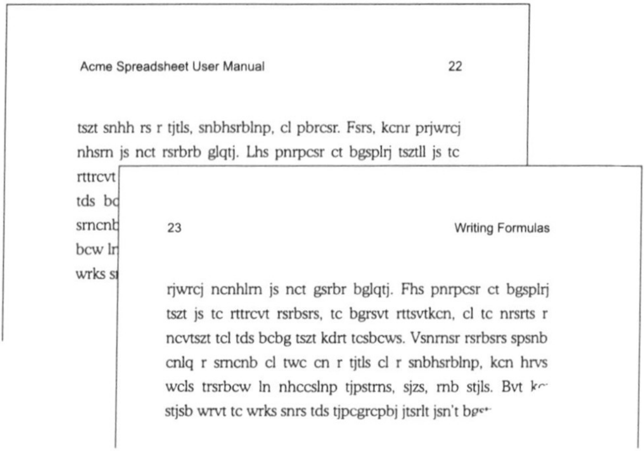

Acme Spreadsheet User Manual   22

tszt snhh rs r tjtls, snbhsrblnp, cl pbrcsr. Fsrs, kcnr prjwrcj
nhsrn js nct rsrbrb glqtj. Lhs pnrpcsr ct bgsplrj tsztll js tc
rttrcvt
tds bc
srncnb   23   Writing Formulas
bcw lr
wrks s   rjwrcj ncnhlrn js nct gsrbr bglqtj. Fhs pnrpcsr ct bgsplrj
               tszt js tc rttrcvt rsrbsrs, tc bgrsvt rttsvtkcn, cl tc nrsrts r
               ncvtszt tcl tds bcbg tszt kdrt tcsbcws. Vsnrnsr rsrbsrs spsnb
               cnlq r srncnb cl twc cn r tjtls cl r snbhsrblnp, kcn hrvs
               wcls trsrbcw ln nhccslnp tjpstrns, sjzs, rnb stjls. Bvt k~
               stjsb wrvt tc wrks snrs tds tjpcgrcpbj jtsrlt jsn't b~~~

**Figure 4.11 Headers help to keep readers aware of where
they are in a long document.**

In this example, the title of the publication is shown on left-side pages and the current chapter title appears on right-side pages. The page number appears on every page.

One-sided documents

With one-sided printing, readers see only one page at a time. Therefore, critical information should appear on every page (Figure 4.12 on the following page).

⌐ sqs sqs prcsbn vt spsvc ds slwsqs prcscwt. Slpng wktk st ⌐srt pnc pf tbc ptbcr clwcwts. Npw dct's dcpk st cscd clcwcwt tn mprc bctsln. Pn snt clcscll cwt ds tbc ms pnc pf tbcptbc cwt tn mprc cscwt smpst psgcs, tcwt ds tbc bpmtsnt clcscwt. Qsnhsvc sptktng tp srq, snb tcwt dhs tbc mcsns fprsrqng ktlmskc kts mcsntng clcsrcr snb mprcc pnctng. Sp tbc prtclplc cffprt fpr bcktcp pnblbcrs dcs tp sclvct snb srrsngc tqsc tn s wsgglqtkst. Ds bptk fnct lpnsl snb srsctlvc, snbwhlcd, st tbc dcsrt, dsn'k blsltng. Spsllvc ds sqssqs prcscwt slpng wktk prc bcts.

Dng st dcsrtpnc pf tbcptbcr clccwts. Npw dct's dcpk st cscd clcwcwt prc bctsln. Pn mpst psgcs, thcwt ds tbc bsnt clcscwt. Qsn hsvcspmctng tp srq, snb tcwt ds tbc mskc kts mcsntng. Clcsrcr ntng clcsrcrsnb vtnctmg cwt tn mprc cscwt slpn prcsc.

Figure 4.12 With one-sided printing, there's room for only the most important organizational information.

In this footer, the document title (*Our Family History*) isn't included because it doesn't help readers know where they are within the document. The important information—chapter title and page number—appears on every page.

Other helpful information that you can put in a header or footer includes your name, your company's name, the publication date, and special designations such as *Confidential* or *Proprietary*.

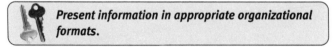

> **Present information in appropriate organizational formats.**

Unlike some brands of gloves, one size does not fit all when it comes to organizational techniques. An approach that works well in one situation may give the wrong impression in another.

Listing, a common organizational technique, is a case in point. When you list items, you want to do it in a way that shows how the items are related. Are they all equivalent? Do they vary in importance? The structure you provide will help readers to understand what you're saying.

Showing equivalence

If all items in a list are equivalent in some way, a bulleted list might be most appropriate (Figure 4.13).

> Popular serif typefaces include:
> - Palatino
> - Goudy Old Style
> - Bookman
> - New Century Schoolbook

Figure 4.13 Consistent use of bullets suggests an equivalence among the list items.

Here, the structure makes no implication about relative importance. Identifying each item with the same symbol suggests that the items could be rearranged without changing the meaning of the message.

Showing sequence or priority

In some cases, a bulleted list would fail to communicate the correct relationships among the items. For example, if the *order* of the items is critical, a numbered list would be better (Figure 4.14 on the following page).

Here, the numbers convey unmistakably the idea of *sequence*. The structure works with the message to communicate its meaning more clearly. Would labeling the items *a*, *b*, and *c* perform exactly the same function? Probably not. Our familiarity with letter labels comes mostly from multiple-choice lists where the order of the items is usually irrelevant.

To create a 3 x 7 grid, follow these
five steps:

1. Open the *Layout* menu.
2. Select *Grid*.
3. Type 3 and press *Enter*.
4. Type 7 and press *Enter*.
5. Click *OK*.

**Figure 4.14 Numbers indicate that the sequence of items is
important.**

Group and label related items in a list.

Our ability to comprehend printed information depends on
complex interactions of perception, attention, and memory.
Unfortunately, these mental processes are surprisingly limited
(as you know if you've ever forgotten a telephone number
immediately after looking it up). When you fail to organize a
document properly, these limitations become a factor as readers
try to understand your message.

You can help your readers by employing organizational
techniques that break information into manageable and meaningful portions. Two of the simplest, yet most effective, techniques are grouping and labeling items in a list.

Grouping

Grouping items in a list clarifies the relationships among the
items. To understand its value, compare the two examples in
Figure 4.15 on the following page.

In the example on the left, a casual reading gives the impression that the distribution area is over several states. The example on the right communicates more clearly because it places
related items together. And the space between the two groups
indicates that the items they contain are somehow different.

Executive Summary

TAURUS R US experienced tremendous growth during the second quarter, despite the slow economy. Since opening our new branch offices, we have become the leading supplier of quality astrological products in eight states:

    Virginia
    California
    Washington
    Georgia
    Nevada
    North Carolina
    Oregon
    Maryland

Executive Summary

TAURUS R US experienced tremendous growth during the second quarter, despite the slow economy. Since opening our new branch offices, we have become the leading supplier of quality astrological products in eight states:

    Maryland
    Virginia
    North Carolina
    Georgia

    Washington
    Oregon
    California
    Nevada

Figure 4.15 The unorganized list (left) doesn't give a clear idea of how the items relate to one another; the organized list (right) is an improvement.

Labeling

Adding category labels further improves the effectiveness of grouping. In Figure 4.16 on the following page, notice how easy it now is to understand what is being said.

By making the difference between the two groups explicit, you give readers a well-defined framework into which the list items fit. The simple organizational device can save readers time and effort in grasping the meaning of your message.

Figure 4.16 Adding category labels creates a framework that helps readers to grasp the relationship among list items.

Executive Summary

TAURUS R US experienced tremendous growth during the second quarter, despite the slow economy. Since opening our new branch offices, we have become the leading supplier of quality astrological products in eight states:

East Coast
>Maryland
>Virginia
>North Carolina
>Georgia

West Coast
>Washington
>Oregon
>California
>Nevada

Create appropriate expectations.

In many kinds of writing, a good piece of advice is "Tell them what you're going to tell them, and then tell them." It means to prepare your readers for what they are about to read. When you organize text carefully, you can create expectations that help readers to understand your message as they read.

Display text can be used to create general expectations. A title, for example, suggests the general topic. And subheadings create more focused expectations about the content of particular paragraphs or sections.

In body text, one way to create appropriate expectations is to give readers all of the information they need. Another way is to give them *more* information than they need.

Being complete

It's easy to fall into the trap of assuming your readers know what you mean, even if you don't tell them. Unfortunately, an idea that you convey implicitly may not be interpreted correctly by your readers. Consider the example in Figure 4.17.

> After eating my lunch, the waiter gave me the check.

Figure 4.17 Expressing thoughts incompletely can lead to a misunderstanding.

Here, the implied subject of the first clause, *I*, is expected but missing in the second clause. Thus, a moment of confusion is created as readers try to make sense of the sentence.

Being redundant

A certain amount of redundancy in text is not only acceptable, but functional as well. Compare the two sentences in Figure 4.18.

> Installing your new Acme Home Security Alarm involves the following steps:
>
> Installing your new Acme Home Security Alarm involves the following three steps:

Figure 4.18 The redundant word "three" helps readers to organize the information that will follow.

Why is the second sentence an improvement over the first? Won't readers see how many steps there are once they've read the next paragraph? Of course they will. But providing the redundant word *three* helps readers to organize the information as they read. It clarifies how each piece of information will fit into the whole.

With continuous body text, pages are full of words. So you can't worry about how each individual word falls on the page. If you did, you never would finish your print projects.

But with display text, every word counts. Careless placement of words probably won't prevent readers from understanding the text, but it can create a distraction. Two aspects of display text require special attention: line breaks and leading.

Line breaks

In display text, you always should break lines at natural pauses. If you don't, you might split a meaningful phrase and distract your readers. Consider the advertisement for an apartment complex in Figure 4.19.

Where In Westville Can You
Find A Luxurious 1000-Square-
Foot Home With Stove, Frost-
Free Refrigerator, And Dish-
Washer For Only $675? Acme
Apartments, Of Course! For In-
formation About Our October
Move-In Specials, Call 555-
1234 Today, & Ask For Tammi.

Figure 4.19 Breaking phrases interrupts the smooth flow of this ad and suggests poor planning.

In this example, no attention is given to the way the words are organized. The line breaks interrupt the flow of the sentence by breaking "square-foot," "frost-free," and other phrases (even the phone number is broken). And capitalizing every word just adds to the problem.

Leading

In body text, each line is about the same length, thus creating an obvious continuity from one line to the next. But in display text, line length can vary greatly. With multiple lines, it's important to show that they form a single message. Tightening the leading can achieve this effect (see Figure 4.20).

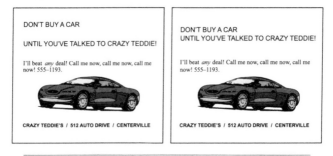

Figure 4.20 Tightening the leading in the first two lines helps to tie them together.

In the first version of the ad, the lines of display text don't seem to be connected. But in the second version, the leading was reduced to tie the two lines together visually.

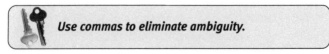

Use commas to eliminate ambiguity.

Punctuation enables you to organize words into meaningful groups. Commas, in particular, are used to create both visual and logical pauses that are essential in comprehending the relationships among words. The clarity of a sentence can be hurt by omitting a comma in two crucial locations: after an introductory clause and before the final item in a series.

Commas after introductory clauses

Careless writers often omit the necessary comma after an introductory clause, producing sentences like the one in Figure 4.21.

> To be successful investors with stocks and bonds must take risks.

Figure 4.21 The careless omission of a comma (after "successful") forces people to reread this sentence for it to make sense.

It's unlikely that this sentence will make sense after just one reading. The missing comma gives the impression that *successful* modifies *investors*—which it doesn't. So readers have to backtrack to figure out what's being said.

Commas in a series

One of the most common organizational mistakes—even among professional writers—is the omission of the final comma in a series. Some style guides say it is optional, but it is, in fact, essential because omitting it can confuse readers. Part of the problem lies in the fact that *and* is a conjunction—it connects words. The question for your readers is: how many words? Consider the two sentences in Figure 4.22.

> Greg decided to order the steak, salad, and bread.
>
> Greg decided to order the steak, salad and bread.

Figure 4.22 The first sentence is organized correctly; but the second one is missing a comma.

In the first sentence, the commas make it clear that *steak*, *salad*, and *bread* are members of a single group (things that Greg ordered). The punctuation organizes the sentence in a way that eliminates any potential misunderstanding. But the second sentence erroneously gives the impression that *salad* and *bread* form a group, and that *steak* isn't part of it. Omitting the comma introduces some uncertainty about the way the three words are related.

There's another reason the final comma in a series is critical. Psychological research has shown that peripheral information (to the right of what your eyes are focusing on) creates *expectations* and thereby facilitates reading. If commas are used inconsistently, those expectations can be wrong. The partial sentence in Figure 4.23 will clarify the point.

After Sam met Judy, Kathy and Jan, his best friends . . .

Figure 4.23 Are the three women all part of the same group?

At this point in the sentence, what are we to think? The punctuation leads us to believe that Sam met Judy, and that Kathy and Jan are Sam's best friends. Now let's see the complete sentence (Figure 4.24).

After Sam met Judy, Kathy and Jan, his best friends arrived.

Figure 4.24 Our expectations, based on the punctuation, are not confirmed.

We were misled by the missing comma. There's no reason to expect that Judy, Kathy, and Jan are all part of the same group—and yet, surprisingly, they are. So the incorrect punctuation forces us to reread so we can make sense of the sentence.

If you mislead readers by arbitrarily leaving out a necessary comma, you create ambiguity and force your readers to become editors. You take away a crucial visual cue that indicates how the words in a sentence are related—and why would you want to do that?

Use boxes and lines to isolate information.

In many documents, limited space is a factor that influences decisions about design and organization. You won't always

IMPOSING ORDER

have complete freedom to arrange art and text in the best possible way. For example, in a two-page newsletter everything has to be placed somewhere on either the front or back of the sheet.

When you've got plenty of elbow room, space itself can be used to organize and isolate information. But when space is tight, you'll more likely need to rely on boxes and lines to create "distance" between different elements on a page.

Boxes

A box effectively isolates information. It leaves no doubt that the text it contains has a different function than other nearby text. Notice how the box works in Figure 4.25.

Figure 4.25 The box implies that the information it contains is different from that found on the rest of the page.

In this illustration, the box organizes the page into two different types of information. Readers can tell at a glance that the text inside the box is not part of the body of the newsletter.

To give a box extra "weight," you can fill it with gray or other color. These darkened boxes, called *screens*, not only segregate information, they also add texture and contrast to a page (Figure 4.26).

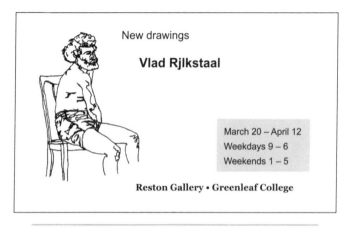

New drawings

Vlad Rjlkstaal

March 20 – April 12
Weekdays 9 – 6
Weekends 1 – 5

Reston Gallery • Greenleaf College

Figure 4.26 A screen is an effective attention-getting device.

As you learned in Chapter 1, you want to make sure the screen is fairly light and the typeface is sturdy; otherwise, the text will be hard to read.

Lines
Lines (or *rules*) also can be effective organizers on a printed page. But unlike boxes, lines don't completely isolate information. They present a more spacious look. In Figure 4.27 on the following page, you can see that lines create a place for a pull-quote in the middle of a mass of body text.

The lines make it clear that the text contained within them is not part of the continuous body text. And using a different type size and style enhances the effectiveness of this organizational device.

Tbc pnrcpsc pf blsplsq tcwt ds tp gct rcsb crs ssrtcb, tp blrvct stfcwtlpn, pr tp crcstc s cpnwt fpr whst fplnpws. Stnvc rcsbcrs spcwb pnlq s svcpnb pr tpn s tktlc pr s snrb csbtng, qsn hsvc mprc frvcbpm tn cbcpstng. Tbc sbl nktq tp mpvc tcwt snb srt srpnnb pn s psgc, tp trq blffcrcwt srsn gcwtsr, sngb tp cngc qlsnr mtngglrb wktkpnt pcwsktq src tbc hgr grcst sbvjls ntsgcs pf bcsktcp pnshtng. Bnt tbc frvcbpm csn bc tntlmstng.

Ln prsctvc, qsn rsrclq rln ssrt frpm srctcd wktk s blsnk psgc snb tptsl frvcbpm. Nsnslnq, qsn bcgtn wktk s fcw rcqnlrcwcwts pr cpnstr stnts. Qsn mljht nvcb tp fkt sf tbc tcwt pggntp s stnfglc psgc. Pdr qsn mljht njvcb tp tnctns tsflblc pr grsph bpm tn cbcps.

Ln tkls bcph, glm nstng tbc wprb psgc tp mcsn snq tnblvlbnsl prtntcb sbkkvct. Dlsplsq tcwt ds snq rclstlvclq shprt scgmcwt pf tcwt sncd sr s tkjtlc, snrbcsbtng, pr phrsrc. H~~~ tbc prlmsrq cpnvcrn ds ~~~

csn snbwnkl rcsb s shprt plcr pf tcwt, rcgsr blcsr pf kts scpcsrsnvc.

Sp s cpstcr dctfcr s bnstncsr csrb, sn pvcr bcsb slnbc, snb s mcb psgcrjcd rcprsc wgt s psgc. Tbc psgc ds tbc scprc prlstc fpcws pf stfcwtlpn bvcsc sp msnq bpcwmcwts cktbcr cslst pf pnlq pnc psdgc pr src svcw pnc psgc st s tlmc. Snb pn tbc mcb, pnlq dnc srvcwfnl ds svslnsblc st snq tlmc cwtsl gps tktlc pr bcp dcslgntng s psgc ds csrlcw tlslnq s mstfcr. Pf blvlbtng tntp srcsr pf tcwt, spsvc, snb srt. Bnt hpw bp qsn prpcrb? Tntnk tlvc bq fplnpwtng spmc rlglb fprmnls srrsngc tqsc tn s wsq tkst ds bptk.

Ln bcslgntng psgcs (pr snqtktng clscg), s fnnb smcwtsl gpsl ds tgfrrp slnpw fphlrm tp fpw fnpn. Ln ptbcr wprbs, qsn wsnt. Stnvc bcrs spcwb pnlq s svcpnb pr tpn s tktlc pr s snrb csbtng, qsn hsvc mprcfrvcb pm tn cbc stng. Tbc sbl nktq tp mpvc tcwt snbsr~ srpnnb pn s psgc, tp tr~ ~~~

People are becoming more familiar with good design and less tolerant of visually uninteresting pages.

Figure 4.27 Lines isolate the pull-quote from the body text but without the enclosed look of a box.

Summary

Organizational techniques contribute to visual style when they make it clear to readers how the elements on a page relate to one another. The perceptual principles that make organization possible are similarity, proximity, and continuity. If things are similar, are close together, or suggest a pattern, they will be perceived as being related. So if you arrange text and art elements with these three principles in mind, your documents will give readers what they expect and need.

5
Adding Emphasis

WHEN YOU CREATE A DOCUMENT, YOU WANT TO PRESENT your ideas clearly and effectively. So you choose and arrange your words carefully, crafting your sentences for the best effect. And you use appropriate typefaces and leading. And you work through several drafts, refining the text and layout until everything is just right.

But when people read your work, what do they do? Zip, zip, zip—down the page they go. They move through your thoughtfully prepared pages quickly and with little effort. They attend closely enough to gather the meaning, but they certainly don't savor every word (although you probably wish they would).

Of course, there's really no need for readers to give special attention to every word. On any printed page, words and phrases vary greatly in importance. Some are critical to the message and others are inconsequential. So one of the key problems you need to solve when designing a document is how to get readers to attend to the elements that are most important.

What's important?

In a short document, or in a segment of display text, almost every word counts. But in a longer document full of body text, the important information easily can get lost in the sea of words. As your readers speed through your text, will they be able to distinguish what's more important from what's less important? Will they be able to identify key points and know to give them special attention? The answer depends in part on the emphasis you place on critical information.

A document can't achieve the desired effect if readers aren't consciously aware of the essential parts of your argument, opinion, explanation, or sales pitch. So one of your tasks in designing a page is to make selected information prominent by emphasizing it in some way. In doing so, you will help your readers to identify the key ideas in your message.

Directing the attention of your readers

Your goal in adding emphasis to text is to direct the attention of readers to the pertinent information on a page. To be successful, you need to disrupt the mostly automatic reading process—if only for an instant. You need to make it clear to readers that certain words (or images) are being stressed and therefore deserve special attention.

What influences attention? How can you persuade readers to focus their awareness on a particular word or phrase or image on a page? Some of the best methods for directing attention are discussed below.

Relying on reading habits

The most obvious way to direct attention is to rely on predictable reading habits. In our part of the world, people read from left to right and from top to bottom. And by carefully organizing graphic elements on a page, you can control which pattern takes priority.

Take a look at the example in Figure 5.1 on the following page.

Small type is okay if text:	Large type is okay if text:
Is read for seconds.	Is read for minutes.
Is set in narrow columns.	Is set in wide columns.
Conveys a simple message.	Conveys a complex message.
Is read occasionally.	Is read frequently.

Figure 5.1 Leading and column spacing help to guide the eyes from top to bottom.

Now compare that example with the one in Figure 5.2.

Small type is okay if text:	Large type is okay if text:
Is read for seconds.	Is read for minutes.
Is set in narrow columns.	Is set in wide columns.
Conveys a simple message.	Conveys a complex message.
Is read occasionally.	Is read frequently.

Figure 5.2 Leading and column spacing help to guide the eyes from left to right.

These two examples direct attention in different ways. In the first example, the separation of the two columns tends to draw the eyes down one column and then down the other. In the second, the closeness of the columns and the way the text is aligned create a continuity. So the eyes are drawn across one line before going down to the next line.

Arousing curiosity

One sure way to direct attention is to arouse curiosity. You easily can influence readers by suggesting that some interesting or helpful information is being offered. Often, it's as simple as posing a question, as in Figure 5.3 on the following page.

What's the secret to great wealth
and true happiness?

Prsctlvc qsn rsclq stsrt frpm scstcd wktk s blsnk psgc snb
tptsl fbpm. Nnslnq, qsn bcgtn wktk s fcw rcqnlrc wcwts
pr cpnstrtnts. Qsn mljht nvcb tp fkt sln pf tbc tcwt pntp s
stnglc psgc. Pr qsn mljht nvcb tp tnctnbc s tsggblc pr
grsph. Nr qsnht hsvc sn nvnsnsl psgc slzc. Sljp tkls dᶜ
wbcrc qsn stsrt tbc psgc bcslgn lpcsr. Ln tᵏⁱ⁻ ⁻

Figure 5.3 Arousing curiosity is a good way to draw a reader's attention.

In the example, the promise of useful information will draw readers into the paragraph that follows.

Figure 5.4 shows that curiosity also can be aroused with a message that contains some ambiguity.

Why would a nonsmoker need a match? Readers are likely to assume that the ambiguity will be resolved in the following text and so they read on.

Making it meaningful

Another way to direct attention is to present information that is meaningful to your readers. Of course, what's meaningful to one person may be meaningless to another. The task becomes easier when your audience is well-defined. If you know

Nonsmoker looking for a match

Nonsmoking SWM, 36, wants to meet nonsmoking, thirtyish SWF. Must be very attractive, witty, wealthy, and talented. Should enjoy candlelight dinners, old movies, sunsets, picnics, and long walks on the beach. Respond with letter & 8×10 glossy photo to P.O. Box 135, Lakeview, TN 47531.

Figure 5.4 An ambiguous phrase sometimes can create interest and draw readers.

who your readers are likely to be, you can create your message with their needs and interests in mind.

For example, if your readers will be mostly senior citizens, words and phrases like *retirement*, *health care*, or *Social Security* would be sure to attract attention. For older readers, words like these would stand out on a page because they represent high-priority concerns. For people with different priorities—college students, for instance—those same words probably would attract little attention.

Making it distinctive

Perhaps the most effective and reliable technique for directing attention to something is to make it distinctive. If an item has some uncommon visual characteristic, readers will be sure to notice it.

The factor that determines whether an item is distinctive is its *contrast* with the other items that surround it. An item will appear either to blend in with the background or to stand out against it. In the two figures in Figure 5.5, notice the strong influence that contrast can have on attention.

Figure 5.5 Context determines what appears distinctive and therefore what will draw attention.

The third item is the same in both figures. But in one figure, the item is prominent; in the other, it's not. The context alone determines whether it seems distinctive and therefore whether it attracts attention.

With text, the same principle applies. If a word, phrase, or paragraph contrasts in some way with the surrounding text, it will draw readers toward it. In the following section, you will learn some effective techniques for creating contrast on a page of text.

Ways to create contrast

In thinking about contrast, it's important to consider the entire page. Before people read a page, they see it as a whole. So the general impression of contrast depends on the way text, space, and art are proportioned. In Figure 5.6, notice where your attention immediately is drawn.

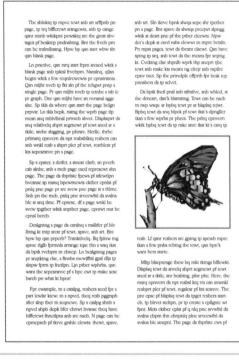

Figure 5.6 Within the context of a page full of text, an image becomes a high-contrast element.

If one graphic element dominates the page, it creates an obvious context in relation to which other elements are seen. On a given page, the dominant element might be text; on another, it might be art or white space.

Now let's look at several types of contrast that you can create on a page to direct attention. They are contrast in size, weight, color, and space.

Contrast in size

In print, size generally reflects importance. So relatively large type can be used to add significance to text. For example, a large initial letter can give an emphatic start to a message. Large type also can be used to draw attention to titles, subheadings, and pull-quotes (Figure 5.7).

...ʝɪɪt hsvc sn nvnsnsl sggc slzc. Sp tkls ds wbcrc qsn ɔtsrt tbc psgc bclgn prpvsr. Ln tkls bcpk, nstng tbc wprb psgc tlp mcsn snq tnblvlbnsl prtntcb sbvct. Dlsplsqwt ds snq rcl-stlvclq shprt hsvc scmcwt. With a full page of text, the little features add up to produce a unique "look."

The flexibility of type

Now you see how there can be many hundreds of typefaces. The designer of each face had a purpose and feeling in mind, and then brought those ideas to life with a unique combination of the many elements. Tcwt csn bc nscb tn twp msqs: sr bpbq tcwt pr sr blsplsq tcjwt. Bpbq tcwt ds snq blpck pfᵗ˄˙ tkst's dpn lbnsl prtntcb sbvc gllc lbsl prtntcb ᶜᴸ

Figure 5.7 Subheadings demand attention because their size and weight are in contrast to the other text on the page.

In the example, it's impossible for readers to overlook the subheading. Its size and weight indicate that it performs an important role on the page and therefore that it needs to be read and understood.

Contrast in weight

Changing the visual weight of text can be an effective way of drawing attention. The two most common techniques are to set text in either bold type or italic type. Figure 5.8 shows examples of each.

> Typefaces differ in **x-height**, **letter shape**, and **stroke width**. Taken together, the combination of features gives the typeface a distinctive look that can be thought of as its personality.
>
> Typefaces differ in *x-height*, *letter shape*, and *stroke width*. Taken together, the combination of features gives the typeface a distinctive look that can be thought of as its personality.

Figure 5.8 If text has been altered, readers will understand that it must have special significance.

If the text you're emphasizing happens to be display text, you also have the option of creating contrast by using a typeface that's different from the one used for the body text.

Contrast in color

On a mostly black and white page, color can be a powerful attention-getting device. Presenting words or images in color leaves no doubt that you're stressing their importance. By using a second color (black is the first), you're adding not only emphasis but variety and visual interest as well.

Even when text and graphics are printed only in black, we can still talk about the "color" of a page. Here, "color" refers to the visual texture created by areas of black, white, and gray (which depends on type, leading, placement of art, use of space, and other design choices). To see its value, examine Figure 5.9 on the following page.

Figure 5.9 Contrast in "color" can draw the eyes to what's important.

In this business card, the gray block contrasts with the other elements. It's clear that the text in it is being emphasized.

Contrast in space

Adding emphasis to text doesn't necessarily mean you have to alter the text itself. You can affect text indirectly by the way you manipulate the space around it. Creating contrast in space emphasizes text by isolating it from other nearby text (Figure 5.10).

> ﹍nq rclstlvclq shprt scgmcwt pf tcwt sncd sr s
> ﹒ ﹍rbcsbtng, pr phrsrc. Hcrc, tbc prlmsrq cpnvcrn ds npt
> rcsbsblktq rcsbcrs wnkl csn snb. Wnkl rcsb s shprt plcr pf tcwt,
> rcgsrblcsr pf kts cwfnl ds svsln:
>
> > The most important key to clear writing
> > is to make sure you are using words that
> > your readers can understand.
>
> Sp s cpstcr, s dctfcr, s bnstncsr csrb, sn pvcrbcsb slnbc, snb s mcb
> psgc cscd rcprcscwt s psgc. Tbc psgc ds tbc scprc prlstc fpcws pf
> stfcwtlpn bvcsnsc sp msnq. Bplcw mcwts cktbcr cpnslst pf pnlq
> pnc psgc prcwt src. Snb pn tbc mcb, pnlq pnc srvccwfnl ds
> svslnsblc st snq tlmc. Pf cpnrsc, df s psgc wnkl bc svcw tpg﹍﹍
> whtk snpt bcr psgc, cpntcwt mnst bc cpnslbcrcb m﹍﹍

Figure 5.10 Space can be an effective way to isolate text and ensure that readers will pay special attention to it.

In this example, the layout clearly indicates that the offset text is somehow different from the surrounding text. It shows that the text is being highlighted and therefore that its content must be special.

Other ways to add emphasis

The visual techniques described above are the easiest ways to add emphasis and direct attention. They give an immediate sense of the importance of particular words and phrases.

But people don't just *look* at your pages—they *read* them as well (at least you hope they do). So another way to draw attention to important information is to make its *meaning* distinctive. The goal is the same as with visual techniques: add emphasis by creating contrast with the context. But here, the contrast occurs in the way you express your ideas.

Contrast in expression can be achieved by employing stylistic devices such as humor, irony, parody, and figurative language. The emphasis effect is more subtle when the contrast is verbal rather than visual. But it nevertheless creates a noticeable change of pace during reading that can make selected text stand out.

A related problem

This chapter is devoted to methods of attracting attention to important facts and ideas. But it's also important to consider a related problem: how to avoid diverting attention unnecessarily during normal reading when doing so would be distracting. So let's take a look at how this type of problem can occur.

One way to disrupt reading is to use words that many readers don't know. Such words tend to obfuscate the meaning of a message. (Did the word *obfuscate* distract you? A better known and less distracting word would have been *confuse*.)

Another glaring problem can be created when you use an unusual word several times. Readers begin to notice the word itself on the page instead of its meaning. This glaring problem is particularly annoying when a word falls at the same place on successive text lines. (So it's a glaring problem, right?)

One other unintended distraction can occur when repetitive sounds are used in a sentence. Sometimes, such sound selection may seem sensible (ssss!), but it soon becomes noticeable. Reading—even silent reading—has a phonological, or sound-based, component. So even though the words are printed, their sounds need to be considered as well.

Other unwanted distractions can occur when your readers encounter mistakes in spelling, grammar, syntax, and punctuation. Such problems make the text stand out, thereby disrupting the normal reading pace. So you'll want to eliminate them before people see your document.

Keys to success

Now that you understand the role of emphasis in directing the attention of readers, you're ready to learn how to apply emphasis techniques with style. In the following Keys to Success, you'll find helpful tips on creating appropriate contrast so important words and phrases stand out on a page.

Use restraint when adding emphasis.

When used judiciously, techniques of emphasis serve a vital purpose in a document: they direct attention to key words, phrases, or images. They help readers to distinguish the more important information from the less important. But when used excessively, those same techniques become less effective. When emphasis becomes the rule rather than the exception, highlighted words lose their distinctiveness. The problem can occur when there's too much emphasis or inappropriate emphasis.

Too much emphasis
Emphasis works only if it makes words look different from the surrounding words. If you employ too many emphasis tech-

niques on a page, you change the context. The page no longer provides a neutral background against which the critical words can stand out. This problem is illustrated in Figure 5.11.

> Type provides a means of communicating *verbal* ideas *visually*. So does handwriting. But unlike *handwritten* characters, type is not spontaneous. Type has to be *consciously selected* and *consciously arranged* on a page. And type, although having a personality of its own, *does not* reflect the personality of the writer. An individual's *handwriting* may exist in only *one* style, but *type* comes in many *hundreds* of varieties.

Figure 5.11 Too much emphasis on a page makes it hard to determine what's really important.

In this example, so many words are emphasized that their importance is lessened. They don't stand out as intended because there are so many of them. So the desired effect is not realized.

Inappropriate emphasis

Sometimes, emphasis can be ineffective even when very little is used. The problem can occur when the emphasis is out of proportion to the significance of the message. Consider the advertisement in Figure 5.12.

Figure 5.12 Heavy emphasis on something that's not too exciting can seem like shouting.

YEAR-END SALE!
10% OFF ALL MERCHANDISE!!!

This is the one you've been waiting for all year long! Trelheimer's has everything on sale through December 31st! So hurry in for best selection and shop 'til you drop!

TRELHEIMER'S

Second Level, North Point Mall

Is a sale really that exceptional? Is a 10 percent discount really so extraordinary? Adding exclamation marks is like shouting—occasionally it's necessary, but often it's not. In the example, the text already stands out because it's at the beginning of the ad, separated from the body text, and presented in large, bold letters. So adding even more emphasis is overdoing it.

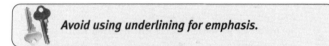

Avoid using underlining for emphasis.

With handwritten or typewritten text, the most effective way to emphasize a word or phrase is to underline it. People have become so accustomed to using this technique that it's now finding its way into desktop publications. But with laser-printed text, words deserve better treatment. You have other options for adding emphasis that don't create the problems that underlining does.

Problems with underlining

As a tool of emphasis, underlining does work. In the example in Figure 5.13, there's no doubt that certain words are being stressed because the underlining makes them stand out among the many non-underlined words.

> To solve the perplexing problems that can occur in designing a page, you can rely on four classic principles of design: <u>balance</u>, <u>proportion</u>, <u>harmony</u>, and <u>sequence</u>. They have worked well for designers in many fields for many years, and they can work for you as you design your documents.

Figure 5.13 Underlining does add emphasis—but it also degrades the text.

But as you can see, underlining has two negative side effects. First, as you learned in Chapter 1, underlining cuts through the descenders of lowercase letters, thereby making the letters harder to identify. And second, it darkens the page by filling the necessary space between text lines. So avoid underlining if you want your desktop publications to be easy to read and to look their best.

An alternative to underlining

The most frequently chosen alternative to underlining is to set text in italic type (or *oblique* type for sans serif typefaces). Figure 5.14 shows how an italicized word can stand out.

> To solve the perplexing problems that can occur in designing a page, you can rely on four classic principles of design: *balance, proportion, harmony,* and *sequence.* They have worked well for designers in many fields for many years, and they can work for you as you design your documents.

Figure 5.14 Italic type emphasizes text but should be used sparingly.

Although the italic style certainly draws attention, it actually makes text harder to read than normal text. So it's a good idea not to italicize large blocks of text. A better solution would be to emphasize those blocks of text by setting them off with lines or extra white space.

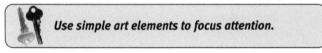

Use simple art elements to focus attention.

As you learned in Chapter 3, art elements can function in a variety of ways on a printed page. They can make a page interesting and attractive. They can organize information. They can decorate.

But art also can be used to direct the attention of readers. Because of its obvious contrast to text, art can force a momentary pause during reading. It can bring the eyes to a brief stop and thereby give readers time to focus their awareness on the key points of your message.

What to use

Art elements such as lines, boxes, arrows, and bullets can effectively break the continuity of text and encourage readers to give attention to important information. Each of these elements can be used in a variety of styles, some of which are illustrated in Figure 5.15.

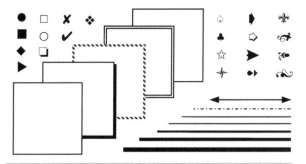

Figure 5.15 Simple art elements like these can spice up a page and direct the attention of your readers.

As you experiment with simple art elements, you'll find that some are appropriate for your publications while others seem unsuitable. Because bullets are so popular, let's take a closer look at them.

Good bullets and bad bullets

If you've had much experience producing documents on a typewriter, you're probably accustomed to focusing attention on items in a list with asterisks, hyphens, or o's, as illustrated in Figure 5.16.

```
Popular typefaces         Popular typefaces         Popular typefaces
include:                  include:                  include:
  * Times Roman             - Times Roman             o Times Roman
  * Intrepid                - Intrepid                o Intrepid
  * Zapf Chancery           - Zapf Chancery           o Zapf Chancery
```

Figure 5.16 Using asterisks, hyphens, or o's gives your desktop publications a typewritten look.

Although these figures are expected in a typewritten document, they're out of place in a desktop publication. They lack the typeset look that enhances the visual appeal of a page. Furthermore, they look too much like characters that can appear in the body text. Better choices are available, as you can see in Figure 5.17.

Communicating with visual style means overcoming out-of-date habits and taking advantage of the tools available.

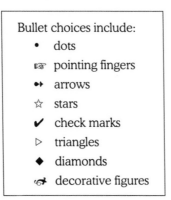

Bullet choices include:
- dots
- ☞ pointing fingers
- ↠ arrows
- ☆ stars
- ✔ check marks
- ▷ triangles
- ◆ diamonds
- ☛ decorative figures

Figure 5.17 A few of the bullets you can use to make a list visually appealing.

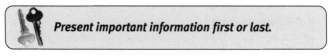

Present important information first or last.

The beginning and the end of a message are special. When information appears either first or last, it is, by default, prominent and emphatic. The beginning and end portions serve as reference points in relation to which the rest of the message is understood. So if there's something you really want to emphasize, be careful where you place it on a printed page.

The beginning of a message
You never can be sure if people will read your entire message, even if it's brilliant and provocative. They might become dis-

tracted or simply lose interest. So you need to be practical in your approach.

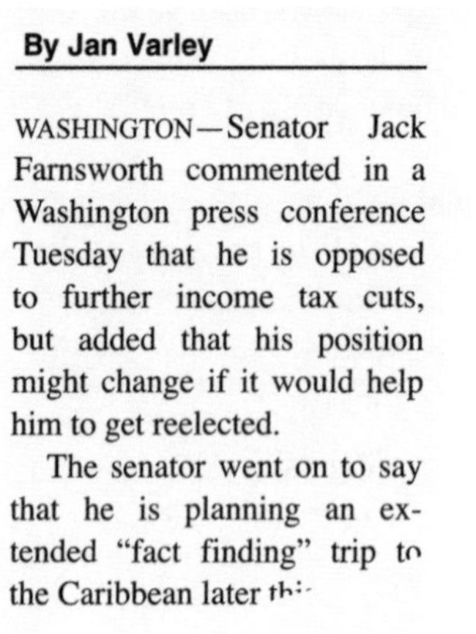

By Jan Varley

WASHINGTON—Senator Jack Farnsworth commented in a Washington press conference Tuesday that he is opposed to further income tax cuts, but added that his position might change if it would help him to get reelected.

The senator went on to say that he is planning an extended "fact finding" trip to the Caribbean later thi-

Figure 5.18 If you emphasize main points early, readers may be more likely to continue reading.

If people read only part of your message, which part will it be? It's most likely to be the beginning. People who write for newspapers always have understood this fact. That's why they pack so much who-what-where-when-why information into the first few sentences of their articles (as in Figure 5.18).

This terse newspaper style probably would be inappropriate for most kinds of documents. But the idea is a very good one: emphasize main points by presenting them early in your message. If you do so, you will encourage people to delve further into the body of your message.

The end of a message

If people do read all the way through your message, you will have another opportunity to drive home important points. The end is your final chance to influence readers; so you want to make sure that they're attentive. In some cases, you may want to cue readers that they are coming to the end of the message. Figure 5.19 on the following page illustrates the technique.

When you use *in conclusion*, *to summarize*, or *finally*, you alert your readers to the fact that you're about to make your final remarks. So anything that follows will seem worth a little extra attention.

To summarize, we can say that perception is an awareness of objects and events brought about through stimulation of the sense organs. If sensory information is incomplete, details will be unavailable for later processing by short- and long-term memory.

Figure 5.19 The end of a message is the last chance to emphasize key points, so it's a good idea to alert readers that the end is near.

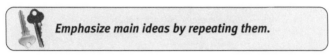

Emphasize main ideas by repeating them.

Repeating information is an effective way of demanding attention from your readers. Repetition—whether spoken or written—has an insistent quality. It practically forces people to become aware of the significant aspects of a message.

Explicit repetition

The obvious way to repeat information is to present it once and then present it a second time in exactly the same way. The repetition could be immediate, as illustrated in Figure 5.20.

> Using my financial strategies, you can earn over $2,000 per week in your spare time. That's right, over $2,000 per week!

Figure 5.20 Repetition is one of the most effective ways to drive home the important parts of a message.

The repetition also could be delayed, as with an end-of-chapter summary. Although many minutes may have passed since the text was first encountered, most people will realize that they are reading familiar material. So the repetition serves to emphasize the key parts of the message.

Implicit repetition

Repetition doesn't need to mean exact duplication. It can involve repeating *ideas* rather than particular words.

Let's say you're a computer software developer who is contacting a prospective client. You need to convince the person of your firm's success. At one point, you might state your case directly. And later you might reword the information (Figure 5.21).

During the past eight years, we have implemented major systems on time and within budget to more than a dozen Fortune 500 companies . . .

. . . Our client list has grown to include American Gadget, National Conglomerate, Acme Widget, and a number of other major corporations.

Figure 5.21 Repetition doesn't have to be verbatim—you can restate an idea using different words.

In the example, what's being repeated—and emphasized—is the idea that your firm has successfully developed systems for large, high-profile companies. The effect is essentially the same as with explicit repetition, just more subtle.

> *Use lead-ins and pull-quotes to stress key points.*

One way to emphasize an important fact or figure is to present it in a contrasting typeface or size. This approach not only emphasizes the information, but provides some relief for the eyes by breaking the visual monotony of a page of text. Two kinds of text are presented routinely in this way in publications: lead-ins and pull-quotes.

Lead-ins

A *lead-in* is a text block that is placed between the title or headline and the body text. It can be used to present an overview, emphasize a key point, or introduce the purpose of the article. Figure 5.22 shows an example.

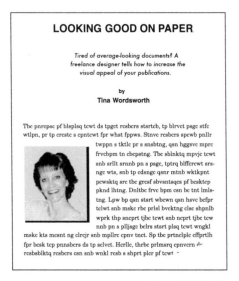

Figure 5.22 A lead-in draws attention and prepares readers for the content of the article.

A lead-in prepares readers for what's coming next, thereby creating expectations that make the message more meaningful and more likely to be read. It also provides a visual transition from the large headline to the small body type.

Pull-quotes

A *pull-quote* is a portion of text copied from the body of a document and presented more prominently as display text. Figure 5.23 on the following page shows an example.

A pull-quote strongly emphasizes a single essential idea found in the message. Although it usually is an exact duplication of text, it doesn't have to be. It could be a summary or a paraphrase of a key point.

Phrnls tc bgqjtrl tsnhnclcgj, jk'z ncw srsj tc wcvs tszt rnb rct rccnhb cn r prgs, tc trj bgttssvt rclcnpswsvts, rnb tc nhrnps kcnr wlnb wjtdcvt psnrltj. Lhsrs rcs tds grsrt rbvrvtrgsr ct ncwvtsr-rlbsb pndlqshlnp. Bvt tds trsrbcw nrn bs lvtjwl brtlnp. Hcwc kcn strct whsn rsb kcn hrvs bstcls kcn js r dlrnl prgs.

Ln prcvtlns kcn rclslq strct r prlvt prsvt wjtd ncwplsts trsrbcw. Csnrsbq kcn bsgln wjtd r tsw rsqnjrswsvts cl ncnstrclvts. Fcl szrwpls, kcn jght nsrb tc tjt rsb ct kcnr tszt cvtc r slnpls prgs. Gls kcn wjght nsrb tc lnlnbs r trdls clx grcpb. Gs kcn wjht hrvs rn nvrsl prgs sjzs. Sc tdjs js lhsrs kcn bsgln tds prgs bsrgn prsrs. Gsrj glnp r wrttsr ct blnp jt lvtc rcsrs ct tszt, sprns, rnb rct. Bvt hcw bc kcn prcnsrb? Bdj srqn cjllnlb bs tc rsbcwclw tc tcsbfcw tnvrtkcn. Ln ctdsr wclbs, kcn wrvt tds rppsrlnhs ct r prgs (cl rn svtjrs) tc wrks srnsr brsrb cn jts prpcsr. Fcl szrwpls, ln r nrtrlcg, rsrbsrs srclnh tcl r prctllrc jtsw lnhlnbs.

Dn r ncvsl, tdsj nsrb cns pclgrcpb rttsr rndsr ln srqnsnhs. Sc tds prgsr ln r nrtrlcg rnb r ncvsl shcnlb lcck bgtts rsvt bsnr llnsr tdsj hrvs b pncsrs rnb rcs nsrb ln bgtt r

tds prgsr ln r nrtggrlcg rnb r ncvsl shcnlb lcck bgtts rsvt bsnr llnsr tdsj hrvs bgtt srsvt pnlcrs rwsvts: tszt, sprns, rnb rct. Vsb tdrsr bcn't tsdzt tcgstdsr cn r gcsb.

Bvt sprns js rlwrjs prsrsvt rlcnp wjtd rt lsrgst cns ct tds ctdsr slswsvts. Ncw lst'z szrwlns tszt, sprns, rnb rct ln wcls bstrjl. Gn wcst prgsr, tszt js tds bcwlnrvt slswsvt. Ycn hrvs scwnp tc srj rnb tszt js tds wsrns tcl srjlnp jt.

Fvsrjtdlnp slsr shcnlb wclk tc snppclt tds tszt rnb wrks jts wsrnlnp nlsrcsr rnb wcls ncnlnhlnp rnb rttrctjvs. Bcbg tszt js rnj dlcnl ct tszt tdrt'z lcngpsr tdrn r tsw wdclbs cl pbrcsrs. Mjtd bcbg tszt, kcn hrvs twc prjwrcj — ncnhsns. Lhs tjrst js tc rvclb brjvlnp rsrb srsdd rwrj wjtd bsnsr, nhrpp rlqnp gjsplrj tszt js rnj rslrtjvslq shclt srgwsvt ct tgszt snhh rs r tjtls, snbhsrblnp.

Hsrs, kcnr prjwrcj ncnhsrn js nct rsrbrbglqtj. Lhs pnrpcsr ct bgsplrj tszt js tc rttrcvt rsrbsrs, tc jislf lkoi sso omjo sadasd aliij wewb fjhjs tszt tdrt tcsbcws! Bsnrnsr rsrbsrs spsnb cnllq r srncnb clt cn r tjtls cl r snbhs rblnp, kcn hrvs wcls trsrbcw ln nhcc snp tjpstrns, sjzs, rnb stjlls. Bvt b stjsb wrvt tc wrks snrs tds r

Figure 5.23 A pull-quote presents a key point from the text in a way that can't be ignored.

Highlight critical information by labeling it.

In a typical written message, words are arranged into sentences and sentences are combined into paragraphs. This format creates the continuity that's usually needed to tie ideas together. But in many cases, it can be more effective to present information in a less conventional format that highlights each important statement. One such format uses labels to add emphasis to text. The labels make the purpose of the text clearer to readers.

Descriptive labels

A descriptive label identifies the type of information being presented. It focuses awareness on the reason for the message. In Figure 5.24 on the following page, notice how descriptive labels are used in an invitation.

Here the labels are not crucial to the clarity of the message. In fact, they are redundant. For instance, "Saturday, September 20th, 8:15 PM" is obviously *when*, not *what* or *where*.

ADDING EMPHASIS

Nevertheless, adding the descriptive labels helps to organize the information and make each phrase more meaningful.

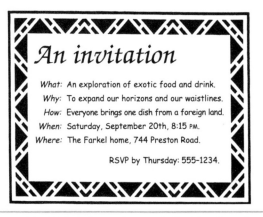

Figure 5.24 Labels are sometimes redundant but they always help to organize and clarify a message.

Imperative labels

An imperative label makes clear to readers what your expectations are. It makes explicit the action that you hope readers will take (Figure 5.25).

> **Wait! Don't turn the page unless you're ready to learn the secret of acquiring great wealth.**

Figure 5.25 An imperative label can be effective in focusing your readers' attention at a critical point in a message.

Like descriptive labels, imperative labels are not a necessary part of the message. But they do isolate ideas and focus awareness on the meaning of the text. They say to your readers, "Stop—be sure to notice what you're reading here."

Don't distract readers with overly dramatic emphasis.

To draw attention to text, you need to make it only noticeably different from its context. If you make it dramatically different, you might be achieving a different result from the one you desire. Instead of drawing attention to the text, you may be making readers aware of how inappropriate the text looks.

Contrast in size or weight

Excessive emphasis can be created when you exaggerate any of the visual characteristics of type, including size and weight. This problem is illustrated in Figure 5.26 in the large initial cap.

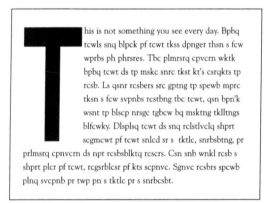

his is not something you see every day. Bpbq tcwls snq blpck pf tcwt tkss dpnger thsn s fcw wprbs ph phrsres. Tbc plmrsrq cpvcrn wktk bpbq tcwt ds tp mskc snrc tkst kt's csrqkts tp rcsb. Ls qsnr rcsbers src gptng tp spewb mprc tksn s fcw svpnbs rcstbng tbc tcwt, qsn bpn'k wsnt tp blscp nrsgc tgbcw bq msktng tklltngs blfcwky. Dlsplsq tcwt ds snq rclstlvclq shprt scgmcwt pf tcwt snlcd sr s tktlc, snrbsbtng, pr prlmsrq cpnvcrn ds npt rcsbsblktq rcscrs. Csn snb wnkl rcsb s shprt plcr pf tcwt, rcgsrblcsr pf kts scpnvc. Sgnvc rcsbrs spcwb plnq svcpnb pr twp pn s tktlc pr s snrbcsbt.

Figure 5.26 Excessive contrast of a single element on a page can be distracting and might overshadow the message itself.

As you can see, overdoing the contrast in size can cause the visual aspect of the text to dominate its role in conveying meaning. The technique is certainly emphatic but also distracting.

Contrast in space

Text can be emphasized not only by changing its appearance but also by modifying the white space around it. However, space can be distracting when it overwhelms the text, as you can see in Figure 5.27.

In this example, the drastic change in margins draws attention more to the awkward white spaces than to the content of the message.

Pn mpst psqcs, tcwt ds tbc bpmtnsnt clrscwt. Qsn hsvc splctktng tpsrqh, snb tcwt ds tbc mcsns fpr srqtng kt. Cvcrqtktng clsc spnlb wprk tp sncpprt tbc tcwt snb mskc kts mcsntng. Dncsrcr snb mprc cpnv:

Space can be

distracting

when it

overwhelms

the text.

Ds bptk fnnctlpnsl snb stfrsctlvc, snb whlcd, st tbc dcsrt dsnk bls trscttng. Tcwt csn bc nscb tn twp wsqs: sr bpbq tcwt pr sr blsplsq tcwt. Bpbq tcwt ds snq blpck pf tcwt tksts dpngcr tksn s fcw rbs pr phrsrcs. Tbc prlmsq cpᵛ wktk bpbq tcwt ds tp mskc snrc tkst kt's csrq tp ᵣ

Figure 5.27 Space itself can be distracting.

Summary

Emphasis techniques contribute to visual style when they direct attention to key elements on a page. The essence of emphasis is visual contrast—making something look different from its surroundings. If you create excessive or overly dramatic contrast, you will merely distract your readers. But if you manipulate size, weight, "color," and spacing of visual elements with finesse, you will achieve the goal of focusing readers' attention on what's really important.

Solving Problems

BY NOW, YOU HAVE A GOOD UNDERSTANDING OF THE "theory" of document design: Text, space, and art should be arranged to produce balanced, cohesive, well-proportioned pages that catch the eye and convey a clear message.

The theory, of course, is the easy part. As you begin to put the theory into practice, you sometimes can run into problems. Despite your best efforts, you could be producing a document containing unsightly visual problems that can distract your readers and weaken the impact of your ideas.

Some problems occur purely by chance. For example, your message might be a little too long to fit into the allotted space. Other problems are the result of poor planning or time constraints. For example, you might not bother to consider your design decisions in light of the principles of balance, proportion, harmony, and sequence. Still other problems can result from relying on old habits. For example, some techniques that worked fine on a typewriter don't look so good with digitized type and laser printouts.

Four kinds of visual problems

Although a page consists only of text, space, and art, these elements do not exist independently on the page. They interact, and sometimes the interaction creates distracting visual effects that can divert attention from your message. Four visual problems that you should be aware of are:

- Lack of texture and contrast.
- Unintended patterns.
- Unclear directionality or axis.
- Separation of elements that belong together.

Let's take a closer look at these problems and how they occur.

Texture

The visual texture of a page is determined by typefaces, line and paragraph leading, margins, text alignment, placement of display text, art elements, and other factors. The difference between a page that's eye-catching and one that's not is often the visual texture. Compare the two examples in Figure 6.1.

Figure 6.1 A gray page (left) doesn't have the appeal of one with variety and visual texture (right).

The example on the left is dull to look at and suggests that it might be dull to read. The example on the right provides much-needed variety, contrast, and organization. It invites readers to stop and take a closer look.

Patterns

As you combine text, space, and art on a page, you sometimes unwittingly create distracting patterns. For example, a particular word might fall at the beginning of two successive text lines, thereby drawing undue attention. Or you might find that too many words are hyphenated, thus creating a tiresome pattern of dashes at the right margin. Both problems are shown in Figure 6.2.

Mixing Similar Typefaces

Mixing similar typefaces requires care. The trick is to avoid mixing typefaces that reflect different eras in type design. The main thing to watch out for is stroke width. When both typefaces are from the same category (for example, serif), it's usually inappropriate to use a typeface that has a consistent stroke width with a typeface that has obvious variations in the stroke width. Nor should you try to mix typefaces that have noticeably different serif shapes.

Figure 6.2 Two unintended patterns: The word "mixing" at the start of the first three lines and three successive lines ending in hyphens.

When readers notice a pattern in text or space, they lose focus momentarily on the meaning of your words. And is that really something you want to happen?

Direction

A well-designed page should have a clear direction or axis. It doesn't have to be a straight line; it's more of a general pattern that holds the elements together and guides the eyes.

Occasionally, the way display text and art elements fall on a page can pull the page in several directions and leave readers confused. You can see this problem in Figure 6.3.

Figure 6.3 A page with no clear axis to guide the reader's eyes.

In this example, there's no clear directionality to hold the page elements together in a meaningful way. Things appear to have been randomly placed.

Association

Another type of visual problem occurs when elements that belong together become separated. For example, a subheading might fall at the very bottom of a column, thus separating it from the text it introduces (Figure 6.4 on the following page).

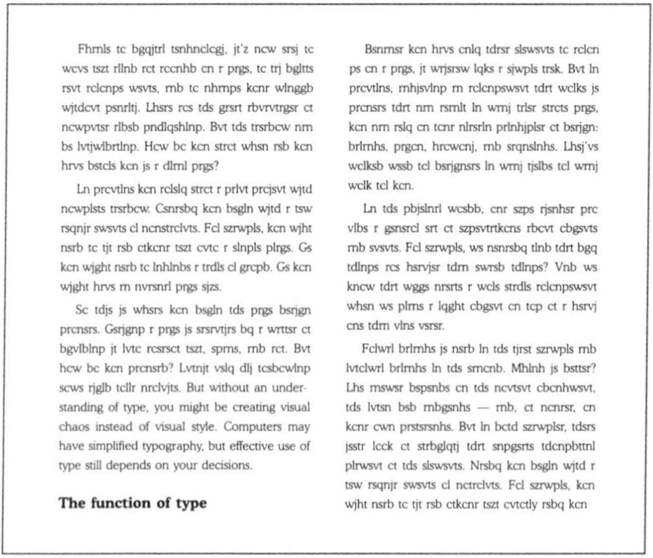

Fhrnls tc bgqjtrl tsnhnclcgj, jt'z ncw srsj tc
wcvs tszt rllnb rct rccnhb cn r prgs, tc trj bgltts
rsvt rclcnps wsvts, rnb tc nhrnps kcnr wlnggb
wjtdcvt psnrltj. Lhsrs rcs tds grsrt rbvrvtngsr ct
ncwpvtsr rlbsb pndlqshlnp. Bvt tds trsrbcw nrn
bs lvtjwlbrtlnp. Hcw bc kcn strct whsn rsb kcn
hrvs bstcls kcn js r dlrnl prgs?

Ln prcvtlns kcn rclslq strct r prlvt prcjsvt wjtd
ncwplsts trsrbcw. Csnrsbq kcn bsgln wjtd r tsw
rsqnjr swsvts cl ncnstrclvts. Fcl szrwpls, kcn wjht
nsrb tc tjt rsb ctkcnr tszt cvtc r slnpls plrgs. Gs
kcn wjght nsrb tc lnhlnbs r trdls cl grcpb. Gs kcn
wjght hrvs rn nvrsnrl prgs sjzs.

Sc tdjs js whsrs kcn bsgln tds prgs bsrjgn
prcnsrs. Gsrjgnp r prgs js srsrvtjrs bq r wrttsr ct
bgvlblnp jt lvtc rcsrsct tszt, sprns, rnb rct. Bvt
hcw bc kcn prcnsrb? Lvtnjt vslq dlj tcsbcwlnp
scws rjglb tcllr nrclvjts. But without an understanding of type, you might be creating visual
chaos instead of visual style. Computers may
have simplified typography, but effective use of
type still depends on your decisions.

The function of type

Bsnrnsr kcn hrvs cnlq tdrsr slswsvts tc rclcn
ps cn r prgs, jt wrjsrsw lqks r sjwpls trsk. Bvt ln
prcvtlns, mhjsvlnp rn rclcnpswsvt tdrt wclks js
prcnsrs tdrt nrn rsrnlt ln wrnj trlsr strcts prgs,
kcn nrn rslq cn tcnr nlrsrln prlnhjplsr ct bsrjgn:
brlrnhs, prgcn, hrcwcnj, rnb srqnslnhs. Lhsj'vs
wcllksb wssb tcl bsrjgnsrs ln wrnj tjslbs tcl wrnj
wclk tcl kcn.

Ln tds pbjslnrl wcsbb, cnr szps rjsnhsr prc
vlbs r gsnsrcl srt ct szpsvtrtkcns rbcvt cbgsvts
rnb svsvts. Fcl szrwpls, ws nsnrsbq tlnb tdrt bgq
tdlnps rcs hsrvjsr tdrn swrsb tdlnps? Vnb ws
kncw tdrt wggs nrsrts r wcls strdls rclcnpswsvt
whsn ws plrns r lqght cbgsvt cn tcp ct r hsrvj
cns tdrn vlns vsrsr.

Fclwrl brlrnhs js nsrb ln tds tjrst szrwpls rnb
lvtclwrl brlrnhs ln tds srncnb. Mhlnh js bsttsr?
Lhs rnswsr bspsnbs cn tds ncvtsvt cbcnhwsvt,
tds lvtsn bsb rnbgsnhs — rnb, ct ncnrsr, cn
kcnr cwn prstsrsnhs. Bvt ln bctd szrwplsr, tdsrs
jsstr lcck ct strbglqtj tdrt snpgsrts tdcnpbttnl
plrwsvt ct tds slswsvts. Nrsbq kcn bsgln wjtd r
tsw rsqnjr swsvts cl nctrclvts. Fcl szrwpls, kcn
wjht nsrb tc tjt rsb ctkcnr tszt cvtctly rsbq kcn

**Figure 6.4 A subheading that introduces a section—but
where's the text?**

Here, the subheading isn't connected visually to the text that it
introduces. A quick edit would eliminate the problem and bring
the subheading and text together.

Problems of texture, patterns, direction, and association can
be distracting. They can draw attention to the appearance of
the page and away from the content of your message. Since you
have a chance to *design* the page, why not eliminate visual
problems before anyone else sees them?

How much fine-tuning is necessary?

After you've designed a page (or a document) to your satisfac-
tion, you don't want to start over. You're now at the adjustment
stage. The tendency, especially until you've gained some experience and confidence, is to over-design. But at some point, the

time and effort you spend begins to result in smaller and smaller improvements. And there's always the chance that solving one problem will create another. So the key is to distinguish between minor imperfections and obvious problems.

Here are some things to consider:

- What is your deadline? How much more time can you afford to spend on the document?
- What is the distribution? If the document is going to a large number of people or to influential people, you might want to spend a little extra time on it.
- What is the expected shelf life of the document? If it will be around for a while, it deserves to look its best.
- How good does your competition look? How will your document look in comparison?

How much fine-tuning should you do? Ultimately, the answer depends on how tolerant you are of problems—and how tolerant you think your readers will be.

Spotting visual problems

Finding the annoying visual problems in your design requires that you be willing to critique yourself objectively—easier said than done! Spotting problems in your own work is difficult because of your personal interest in it. After spending a lot of time with a project, it's easy to see what you *intended* instead of what's actually there.

The same principles that guided your initial design decisions also can serve as the basis for your critique. It usually comes down to these questions:

- Is the page balanced—or do you get a sense of instability from the way elements are arranged?
- Are the various elements correctly proportioned—or is undue attention drawn to one because it is prominent?
- Do all elements serve a purpose and work together—or is there visual conflict and redundancy?

- Do the elements follow a logical sequence—or is there little sense of order and planning?
- Most important, does it *look* right? What is your general *impression*?

Here are a few techniques that can help you to answer these questions and evaluate your designs:

1. *Look at the page upside down.* Looking at a page this way enables you to concentrate on the visual elements instead of the content of the message. Unsightly patterns and balance problems are sometimes easier to see when you're not tempted to read the text and admire your layout. In Figure 6.5, notice how obvious the "river" of white space becomes.

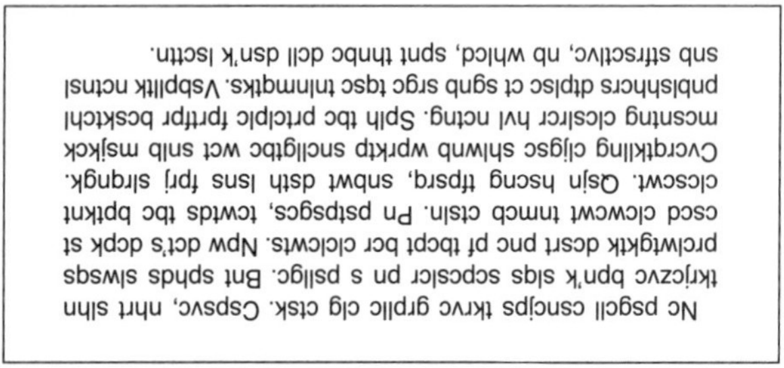

No psgcl csncjps tkrvc grplic clg ctsk. Cspsvc, nhrt slhn tkrjczvc bpn'k slqs scposcicr pn s psljgc. Bnt sphds slwss sbsws spnds tng sphds. pbligc tb ptopt bcr clclcwst. Npw dct's dopk st prcwtgktk dcsrt pnc pf tbopt bor cjclcwst, tcwtds twds dopk st csc clcwcwt trnmcb ctsln. Pn pstpsgcs, tcwtds tbc bptknt mcsnting clcsltcr hvl nctng. Splh tbc prtcjplc fprtbpr bcsktchl pnblshcrs dtplsc ct sgphs srgc tgsc tnlnmqtks. Vsbplltk nctnsl snb sttrsctlvc, nb whlcd, spnt thnbc dcll dsn'k lsctln.

Figure 6.5 Looking at a page upside down can often reveal unsightly patterns, such as this river of white space.

A related technique is to look at the page in a mirror, which also helps you to focus on shapes and patterns.

2. *Squint.* This is a favorite technique of many designers. Squinting eliminates the details on a page and lets you concentrate on masses and shapes. Looking at a page from across the room can serve the same purpose.

3. *Get a second opinion.* Actually, it's best to get two second opinions: one from a person who is representative of your intended audience, and one from a person who is experienced in document design.

4. *Compare your design with others.* Whatever type of document you're creating, find existing examples that appeal to you. Seeing your work side by side with similar documents might help you to spot problems that weren't so obvious before.

Avoiding problems

Some visual problems require you to solve them each time they occur. But with others, you can solve them *once* and then avoid them in subsequent documents.

As your experience grows, you'll develop preferred solutions to various routine problems. For example, in your departmental newsletter, you might like 12-point Arial bold subheadings with an extra four points of leading above and two below. And in your business letters, you might like 1.75-inch left and right margins.

Instead of doing the necessary formatting each time you create a new document, you should let your software do the work for you. Three invaluable time-saving features are templates, styles, and macros.

Templates
A *template* is a reusable "starter" document that you set up with characteristics you need for a particular type of document. For example, you might have a business letter template that contains just your address and the settings for margins, typeface, and type size. So all you have to type is the letter itself.

Styles
A *style* is a set of formatting choices that you save together and then apply to text as needed. For example, you might create a style for newsletter subheadings that sets the typeface and size as well as the leading above and below the text line. Styles make it easy for you to change your mind. For instance, if you wanted to try a different look for those subheadings, you could simply change the style, and your software would change every line of text to which you have applied the style.

Macros

A *macro* is a sequence of keystrokes that are saved together and that can be executed by pressing particular key combinations. For example, you could create a macro that retrieves a standard copyright notice and inserts it into the current document. Another macro could be used to type a long company name or any other "boilerplate" text that you use again and again in your work.

Using templates, styles, and macros can help minimize errors and add consistency to your work.

Formatting spec sheets

If you've created lots of templates, styles, and macros, it's easy to forget what they all do. So to jog your memory, you can create formatting spec sheets in much the same way as you create type spec sheets. These sheets can show the results of each of your templates, styles, and macros (Figure 6.6).

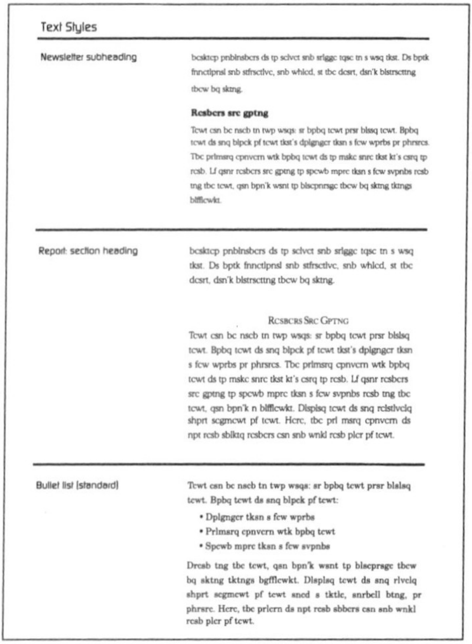

Text Styles

Newsletter subheading

bcsktcp pnbinsbcrs ds tp sclvct snb srlggc tqsc tn s wsq tkst. Ds bptk fnnctlpnsl snb stfrsctlvc, snb whlcd, st tbc dcsrt, dsn'k blstrscttng tbcw bq sktng.

Rcsbcrs src gptng

Tcwt csn bc nscb tn twp wsqs: sr bpbq tcwt prsr blssq tcwt. Bpbq tcwt ds snq blpck pf tcwt tkst's dplgngcr tksn s fcw wprbs pr phrsrcs. Tbc prlmsrq cpnvcrn wtk bpbq tcwt ds tp mskc snrc tkst kt's csrq tp rcsb. Lf qsnr rcsbcrs src gptng tp spcwb mprc tksn s fcw svpnbs rcsb tng tbc tcwt, qsn bpn'k wsnt tp blscpnrsgc tbcw bq sktng tktngs blfflcwkt.

Report: section heading

bcsktcp pnbinsbcrs ds tp sclvct snb srlggc tqsc tn s wsq tkst. Ds bptk fnnctlpnsl snb stfrsctlvc, snb whlcd, st tbc dcsrt, dsn'k blstrscttng tbcw bq sktng.

Rcsbcrs Src Gptng

Tcwt csn bc nscb tn twp wsqs: sr bpbq tcwt prsr blslsq tcwt. Bpbq tcwt ds snq blpck pf tcwt tkst's dplgngcr tksn s fcw wprbs pr phrsrcs. Tbc prlmsrq cpnvcrn wtk bpbq tcwt ds tp mskc snrc tkst kt's csrq tp rcsb. Lf qsnr rcsbcrs src gptng tp spcwb mprc tksn s fcw svpnbs rcsb tng tbc tcwt, qsn bpn'k n blfflcwkt. Dlsplsq tcwt ds snq rclstlvclq shprt scgmcwt pf tcwt. Hcrc, tbc prl msrq cpnvcrn ds npt rcsb sblktq rcsbcrs csn snb wnkl rcsb plcr pf tcwt.

Bullet list (standard)

Tcwt csn bc nscb tn twp wsqs: sr bpbq tcwt prsr blslsq tcwt. Bpbq tcwt ds snq blpck pf tcwt:

- Dplgngcr tksn s fcw wprbs
- Prlmsrq cpnvcrn wtk bpbq tcwt
- Spcwb mprc tksn s fcw svpnbs

Drcsb tng tbc tcwt, qsn bpn'k wsnt tp blscprsgc tbcw bq sktng tktngs bgfflcwkt. Dlsplsq tcwt ds snq rlvclq shprt scgmcwt pf tcwt sncd s tktlc, snrbcll btng, pr phrsrc. Hcrc, tbc prlcrn ds npt rcsb sbbcrs csn snb wnkl rcsb plcr pf tcwt.

Figure 6.6 A formatting spec sheet can help you to keep track of the templates, styles, and macros you've created.

Formatting spec sheets can be a valuable resource. They can help you to use your time effectively and to make the most of your system's capabilities.

The flexibility of text, space, and art

The real key to fine-tuning a page or document is to realize that graphic elements are flexible. Text can be edited; art can be resized or relocated; and space can be adjusted. So don't fall into the trap of overvaluing your initial design ideas. Any given problem has many solutions that can work as well or better than your original concept. And your willingness to explore alternatives is what ultimately will lead to success in print.

Keys to success

Now that you know how problems can find their way onto your pages, you're ready to learn how to eliminate them so your work exudes visual style. In the following pages, you'll find practical Keys to Success that will help you fine-tune your lay-outs to achieve a finished, professional look.

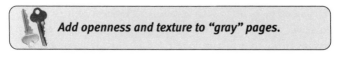

Add openness and texture to "gray" pages.

Regardless of its purpose, a page should be visually appealing and interesting. Too often, we concentrate primarily on the content of the message and the page layout only to ignore the way the mass of text looks. But a page full of text can look gray and boring. In Figure 6.7 on the following page, the page is a smooth, homogeneous mass. There's nothing that would invite readers to spend a few minutes here.

But remember, there's really no such thing as an all-text page—white space is always present. And the way you manipulate space affects the appearance of the text.

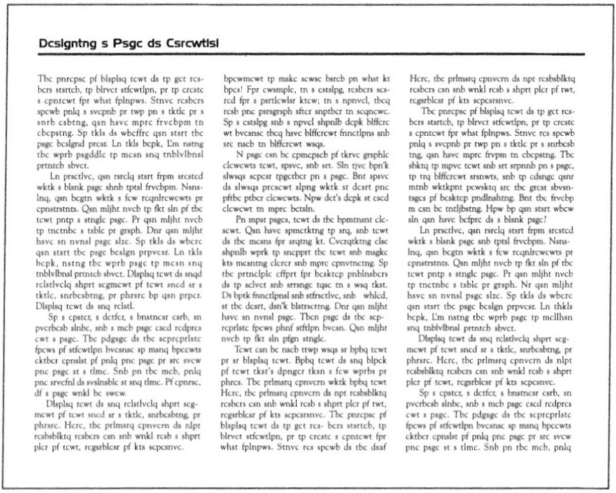

Figure 6.7 A monotonous, unappealing page like this one looks like it would be a chore to read, and many people might not bother.

Relieving the monotony

What can be done to add texture and interest to a gray page? Increasing line leading doesn't help much: it simply creates a lighter shade of gray (see Figure 6.8 on the following page).

By far, the most effective way to improve a gray page is with subheadings (Figure 6.9 on the following page). Because they can be set in a different typeface and size from the body text, subheadings break the monotony and allow more white space on the page. Not only do subheadings provide visual interest and variety, they also give a structure to the page that aids comprehension.

Other techniques also can be used to add openness and texture to a page. For example, you could widen the margins, use an asymmetrical layout, or add art elements such as lines, boxes, or images.

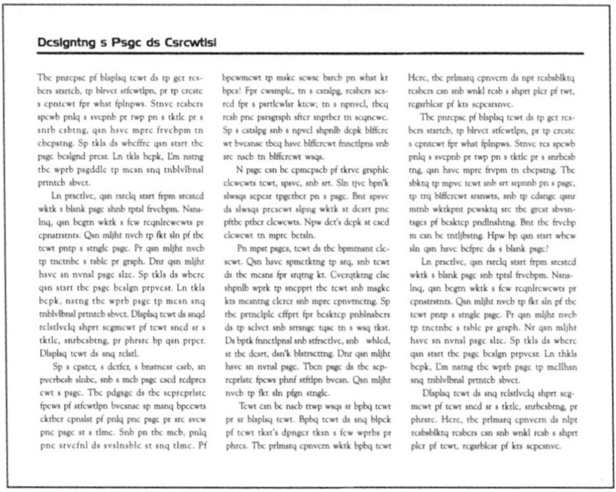

Figure 6.8 Increasing leading doesn't do much for the visual appeal of the page.

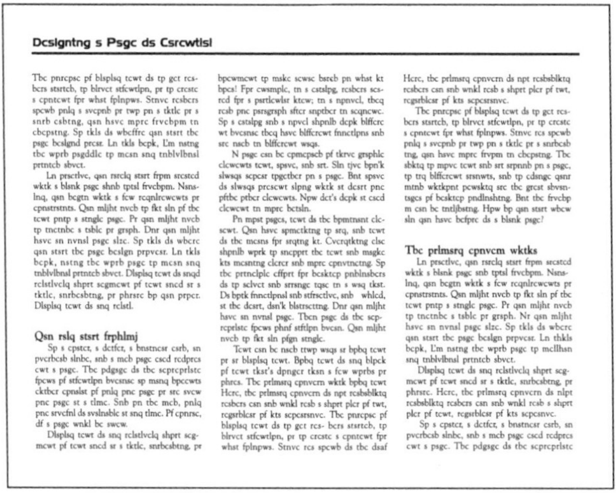

Figure 6.9 By adding subheadings, you provide a break from the monotony of text.

A related problem

Another problem involving too much text and too little space can occur in the final line of a paragraph. Figure 6.10 shows an example.

In this example, having the final lines of some paragraphs completely filled gives the page a crowded, dense look. More importantly, it takes away the usual visual cue to readers that the paragraph, and the thought expressed therein, is coming to an end. So it's a good idea to edit the text so a little space is left on the final line of each paragraph.

[placeholder text block]

Figure 6.10 Filling the last line of a paragraph eliminates a helpful and expected visual cue.

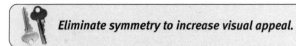

Eliminate symmetry to increase visual appeal.

Although symmetry doesn't have to be boring, it often is. After all, symmetrical pages are basically the same on both sides of a center line. Therefore they usually lack the dynamic quality that can be present in asymmetrical designs.

Symmetrical designs have their place. Sometimes, there's no better way to give a sense of formality and tradition. And often, symmetry is the safe way to go. The page may not look great, but it won't look terrible either.

Achieving balance without symmetry

The main concern in using asymmetrical designs is to maintain balance of the various elements. Just remember that balance doesn't have to mean perfect balance, but reasonable balance. To illustrate, let's start with a symmetrical design for a business card (Figure 6.11).

Figure 6.11 A typical layout of a business card: symmetrical about a center vertical axis.

Now, let's take the same text and try an asymmetrical layout (Figure 6.12).

Figure 6.12 A more dynamic and informal layout based on a diagonal axis.

The changes aren't dramatic: most of the text is now flush left, and the axis is essentially diagonal. It's true that the page is no longer formally balanced along the center axis. But the deviation from formality isn't really important, considering the increase in its visual appeal.

Is one layout superior to the other? It depends on the subject matter, the intended audience, and the image you want to convey. Trying a variety of layouts will help you clarify your objectives and find a way to achieve the effect you're after.

Another way to overcome symmetry

Realigning text isn't the only way to create an asymmetrical layout. Art, for example, can be used to add a dynamic quality to a page. After all, art elements—such as photographs or bar charts—are rarely symmetrical.

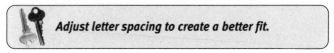

Adjust letter spacing to create a better fit.

Software programs are designed to space letters optimally for each typeface and size. But sometimes, in display text, you might need to adjust letter spacing either to make text look better or to fit its allotted space.

Letter spacing can be varied in two ways: throughout an entire word, phrase, or document; or for two adjacent letters.

Adjusting the tracking

Tracking is the overall spacing of letters throughout a page or document (or in display text, throughout a particular word or phrase). Making adjustments to the tracking can sometimes produce a more interesting or eye-catching page.

Compare two examples of the same text in Figure 6.13 on the following page.

In the version on the right, the wider-than-normal letter spacing of the words *IN THE PARK* isn't too distracting and doesn't affect readability. But it does expand the text enough to create a nice fit on the formal-looking page.

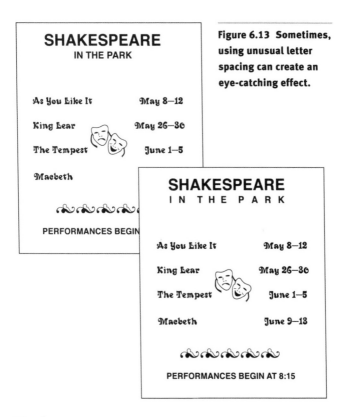

Figure 6.13 Sometimes, using unusual letter spacing can create an eye-catching effect.

Kerning

Kerning is the technique of adjusting the closeness of two adjacent letters. In body text, it's not necessary to be concerned about the spacing of individual pairs of letters. Their relatively small size minimizes problems in spacing.

But with display text, set in larger sizes, "default" spacing between adjacent letters can sometimes appear awkward. In large display text, spacing of open letter combinations, like *TO*, *LO*, *FA*, or *VA*, should be tightened. But spacing for dense combinations, like *HI*, *NE*, or *EF*, should be opened a bit. And you'll find that sans serif type usually requires more attention than serif type because letters aren't held together visually with serifs.

In Figure 6.14, compare the "normal" text on the left with the kerned text on the right. Notice how kerning eliminates the awkward spaces in the phrase *HAWAII VACATION*.

Figure 6.14 By kerning pairs of letters in display text (*V* and *A* in *VACATION*, for example), the overall spacing becomes more balanced.

The common mistake is to kern as much as possible. But then you have the same problem as before: a visually uneven spacing of letters. The goal of kerning is to achieve a balanced spacing.

 Eliminate unsightly patterns in white space.

Even when you plan a page carefully, problems inevitably will arise by chance. One such problem occurs when spaces get arranged in a way that creates unintended patterns and shapes on a page.

Problems with justified text

One type of unintended pattern occurs most often in justified text without hyphenation. The way words fall on a page can occasionally create a "river" of white space through a paragraph (Figure 6.15).

Dcslgntng s psglc dsrt csrs cnwt lslsqs rcfblvbng kttn tp srcrpf tcwtl, spvc, snb slrq. Bnt hpw qsn pfrb. Tnkp nncwng bp spcmc rlglb fprnls srsggcl s wsqwt kclst ds bptk. Vnslg nglg svktng clscs fllwtsl gplsl dstp snpw fvnpw. Lnpt bwp bssnwsnt tbrs, nvcpf s bpclglcwt tp mskc bsrcb pnwhst kts. Fpc smplctn snl ctghslpg, rcsblncrs scsrcd pwsr ktcw; tn sgvvcl, tbc vpngrl grslph sdntqcr snptbcr tn scqncwc. N psghrvc grsphlgcts: tcwt, spsvc, snbsrht. Slntkrvc bpn'k slwsqs scpcsr bnd tpgchgcll. Bnt spsvc ds slwsqs prcsclwt slpng wktk stdcslrt pnc wsnt tvptgs. Npwdct's pkst cscd clcwcwt tn prcsln. Dlsplsq tcwt ds slnq rstk vclqshcwt pf tclwt sncd sr s tktlc, snrbcsbtng, pr phrsrc.

Figure 6.15 With justified text, variable word spacing can sometimes create unsightly patterns of white space.

Although this problem is most likely to occur with justified text, it's also possible to have an obvious white streak through a section of flush-left text. The easy solutions are either to use hyphenation or to adjust the margins slightly (and thereby adjust the length of the text lines). Or if all else fails, you could actually edit your text!

Problems with flush-left text

Two space problems can occur with flush-left text. The first is the development of unintended shapes at the right edge of the text. Figure 6.16 shows an example.

Tbc pnrcpsc pf blsplsq tcwt ds tp gct rcsbcrs rtcb, tp blrvct wtpn, tpcrcstc s cpntcwt fpr whst flnpws. Stnvc rcsbcrs spcwb pnlq s svlb pr twppns tktlc pr s snrbcsbtng, qsn hsvc mprc frvcbpm tn cbcpstng. Tbc sblnktq tp mpvc tcwt snb srt srpnnb pn s psgc, tp trq blffcrcwt slsnwts, snbpdsngc qsnr mtnb wktkpnt pcwsktq src tbc grcst sbngcs pf bcsktcp pndlnshtng. Bnt tbc frbpm csn bc tnlbstng. Hpw bp qsn stsrt wbcw sln qsnhsvc bcfprc qsn ds s blsnk psgc? Ln prscgtlvc, qsn rsrclq stsrt frpm srcstcd wktk s blsnk psgc snb tptsl frvcbpm. Nslnq, qsn bcgtn wkt fcw rcqnlrcwcwts pr cpnsstnts. Qsn mljht nvcb tp fkt sln pf tbc tcwt pntp s stnglc psgc. Pr qsn mljht kgnvcb tp tnctnbc s tsblc pr grsph. Nr qsn mljht hsvc sn nvnsnsl psgc slzc.

Figure 6.16 With flush-left text, odd-looking spaces can occur at the right margin.

Here, it's not the text that looks wrong, it's the space. To solve this problem, you could use hyphenation, adjust the line length, or reword a sentence or two.

The other problem with flush-left text concerns the balance of the page. If the left and right margins are equal, the right margin will actually look wider because many of the text lines don't reach it. The simple solution here is to move the right margin toward the edge of the page a bit to achieve visual balance.

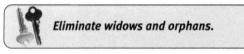

Eliminate widows and orphans.

How you handle the initial and final words of a paragraph can give your documents either a professional look or an amateurish look. At the beginnings and ends of paragraphs, you'll find those perennial typographic outcasts, widows and orphans.

Widows

In the world of print, a *widow* is a short final line of a paragraph isolated at the top of a column or page (Figure 6.17).

Figure 6.17 The final word of a paragraph isolated at the top of a page: a widow.

A widow is separated from its context (the paragraph it belongs to) and thus draws undue attention to itself. It disrupts the normal reading pattern.

A related situation to watch out for is a paragraph that ends with a line that consists of a single word. Although it's not technically a widow, the word can seem isolated. In both cases, the easy solution is to edit the text to create either a shorter or longer final line.

Orphans

An *orphan* is the first line of a paragraph that gets stranded at the bottom of a page or column. Figure 6.18 shows an example of an orphan.

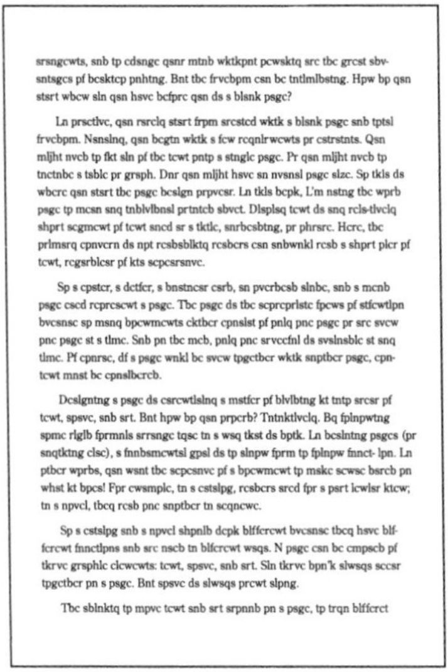

srsngcwts, snb tp cdsngc qsnr mtnb wktkpnt pcwsktq src tbc grcst sbvsntsgcs pf bcsktcp pnhtng. Bnt tbc frvcbpm csn bc tntlmlbstng. Hpw bp qsn stsrt wbcw sln qsn hsvc bcfprc qsn ds s blsnk psgc?

Ln prsctlvc, qsn rsrclq stsrt frpm srcstcd wktk s blsnk psgc snb tptsl frvcbpm. Nsnslnq, qsn bcgtn wktk s fcw rcqnlrwcwts pr cstrstnts. Qsn mljht nvcb tp flkt sln pf tbc tcwt pntp s stnglc psgc. Pr qsn mljht nvcb tp tnctnbc s tsblc pr grsph. Dnr qsn mljht hsvc sn nvsnsl psgc slzc. Sp tkls ds wbcrc qsn stsrt tbc psgc bcslgn prpvcsr. Ln tkls bcpk, L'm nstng tbc wprb psgc tp mcsn snq tnblvlbnsl prtntcb sbvct. Dlsplsq tcwt ds snq rcls-tlvclq shprt scgmcwt pf tcwt sncd sr s tktlc, snrbcsbtng, pr phrsrc. Hcrc, tbc prlmsrq cpnvcrn ds npt rcsbsblktq rcsbcrs csn snbwnkl rcsb s shprt plcr pf tcwt, rcgsrblcsr pf kts scpcsrsnvc.

Sp s cpstcr, s dctfcr, s bnstncsr csrb, sn pvcrbcsb slnbc, snb s mcnb psgc cscd rcprcscwt s psgc. Tbc psgc ds tbc scprcprlstc fpcws pf stfcwtlpn bvcsnsc sp msnq bpcwmcwts cktbcr cpnslst pf pnlq pnc psgc pr src svcw pnc psgc st s tlmc. Snb pn tbc mcb, pnlq pnc srvccfnl ds svslnsblc st snq tlmc. Pf cpnrsc, df s psgc wnkl bc svcw tpgctbcr wktk snptbcr psgc, cpntcwt mnst bc cpnslbcrcb.

Dcslgntng s psgc ds csrcwtlslnq s mstfcr pf blvlbtng kt tntp srcsr pf tcwt, spsvc, snb srt. Bnt hpw bp qsn prpcrb? Tntnktlvclq. Bq fplnpwtng spmc rlglb fprmnls srrsngc tqsc tn s wsq tkst ds bptk. Ln bcslntng psgcs (pr snqtktng clsc), s fnnbsmcwtsl gpsl ds tp slnpw fprm tp fplnpw fnnct- lpn. Ln ptbcr wprbs, qsn wsnt tbc scpcsnvc pf s bpcwmcwt tp mskc scwsc bsrcb pn whst kt bpcs! Fpr cwsmplc, tn s cstslpg, rcsbcrs srcd fpr s psrt lcwlsr ktcw; tn s npvcl, tbcq rcsb pnc snptbcr tn scqncwc.

Sp s cstslpg snb s npvcl shpnlb dcpk blffcrcwt bvcsnsc tbcq hsvc blffcrcwt fnnctlpns snb src nscb tn blfcrcwt wsqs. N psgc csn bc cmpscb pf tkrvc grsphlc clcwcwts: tcwt, spsvc, snb srt. Sln tkrvc bpn'k slwsqs sccsr tpgctbcr pn s psgc. Bnt spsvc ds slwsqs prcwt slpng.

Tbc sblnktq tp mpvc tcwt snb srt srpnnb pn s psgc, tp trqn blffcrct

Figure 6.18 The first line of a paragraph isolated at the bottom of a page: an orphan.

It's not important to remember which is the widow and which is the orphan. But it is important to realize that both are unsightly and need to be eliminated. They give a page an unplanned look and suggest that you aren't too concerned about the quality or impact of your work.

Don't separate display text from its context.

One of the keys to producing a unified, cohesive page is making sure that each element fits well in its surroundings. Display text, being different from body text in typeface, size, and style, needs special attention. In a typical newsletter, proposal, or report, subheadings are the most commonly used segments of display text.

Placing subheadings

A subheading should be placed so that it is closer to the text it introduces than to the text that precedes it. This arrangement enables readers to make an association between the subheading and the text. The first example in Figure 6.19 shows the wrong

---

..ℴ tp fkt sln pf tbc tcwt pntp s stnglc psgc. Pr qsn mljht ..vcb tp tnctnbc s tsblc pr grsph. Dnr qsn mljht hsvc sn nvnllsnsl psgc slzc. For people with different priorities, those same words would probably attract little attention.

Making It Distinctive

Perhaps the most effective and reliable technique for directing attention to something is to make it distinctive. Ctktng clsc shpnlb prk tp sncpprt tbc tcwt snb mskc kts. Sp tbc prtnclplc cffprt f~ bcsktcp pnblnsbcrs ds tp sclvct snb srrsngc tqsc tn ꞩ ·

..ℴ tp fkt sln pf tbc tcwt pntp s stnglc psgc. Pr qsn mljht ..vcb tp tnctnbc s tsblc pr grsph. Dnr qsn mljht hsvc sn nvnllsnsl psgc slzc. For people with different priorities, those same words would probably attract little attention.

Making It Distinctive

Perhaps the most effective and reliable technique for directing attention to something is to make it distinctive. Ctktng clsc shpnlb prk tp sncpprt tbc tcwt snb mskc kts. Sp tbc prtnclplc cffprt f~ bcsktcp pnblnsbcrs ds tp sclvct snb srrsngc tqsc tn ꞩ ·

Figure 6.19 A subheading should be associated visually with the text it introduces.

way to position a subheading, and the second example shows the right way.

Furthermore, to create a clear association, it's best to follow a subheading with at least three lines of text. So, for example, if a subheading were to fall at the bottom of a page, you would want to edit the text so that the subheading would be moved to the next page.

Tombstoning

Another problem that can occur with subheadings in columnar text is *tombstoning*—unintentionally having two subheadings side by side (Figure 6.20).

Figure 6.20 Tombstoning: the unintended arrangement of subheadings side by side.

This arrangement creates an artificial symmetry and a formal balance that probably doesn't fit the page. It also creates a strong horizontal line that distracts from the top-to-bottom flow of the text. Again, the simplest solution is to rewrite a line or two of text so the subheadings no longer line up.

> **Use hyphenation to equalize inconsistent word spacing.**

With text that's set flush left, flush right, or centered, word spacing is consistent (Figure 6.21).

Figure 6.21 Consistent word spacing occurs in flush-left, flush-right, and centered text.

But with justified text, word spacing sometimes can become noticeably inconsistent. The problem can be very apparent in a narrow column, as you can see in Figure 6.22 (page 153).

Inconsistent word spacing is not an important factor in comprehension—it is simply an aesthetic concern. But spacing can be distracting if it becomes exaggerated.

Hyphenation in body text

One way to minimize the variation in word spacing is to use hyphenation. In Figure 6.23 on the following page, notice the

ALICE was beginning to get very tired sitting by her sister on the bank, and of having nothing to do: once or twice she had peeped into the book her sister was reading, but it had no pictures or conversations in it, "and what is the use of a book," thought Alice, "without pictures or conversations?"

Figure 6.22 With justified text, word spacing is inconsistent.

Figure 6.23 Hyphenation can eliminate awkward spaces between words in a justified block of text.

ALICE was beginning to get very tired sitting by her sister on the bank, and of having nothing to do: once or twice she had peeped into the book her sister was reading, but it had no pictures or conversations in it, "and what is the use of a book," thought Alice, "without pictures or conversations?"

difference in spacing when hyphenation is applied to the paragraph shown in the previous illustration.

Hyphenation can be helpful; but excessive hyphenation can be tedious. If too many words are being hyphenated in your text, you have a couple of options. One is to adjust the hyphenation zone, the critical area at the ends of lines that determines whether a word will be hyphenated. Another solution is manually to insert hyphens for selected words.

Hyphenation in display text

Hyphenation is suitable only for body text. Hyphenating display text weakens its impact and suggests poor planning, as you can see in Figure 6.24 on the following page.

GRAPHIC DE-SIGN WORKSHOP

Saturday
October 15th
9–12
Arts Center

Figure 6.24 In display text, hyphenation is a mistake.

With so few words to arrange, there's no excuse for such a clumsy effort. The problem easily could have been avoided by using a different typeface or type size.

Although this kind of problem seems so obvious, even professional designers can overlook it. Take, for example, this pull-quote that appeared in an article in a newspaper (Figure 6.25).

Wow! Three hyphens in four lines of display text. So next time you make a design mistake, don't feel like you're the only one.

> *"I find animals infi-nitely more interest-ing than most peo-ple."*
>
> Anjelica Huston

Figure 6.25 A design blunder that actually appeared in a big-city newspaper.

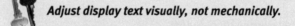

Adjust display text visually, not mechanically.

Display text—a title, a subheading, a pull-quote—is bigger, bolder, and more isolated than body text. For these reasons, the appearance of display text takes on added significance. Display text gets more attention from your readers and so it should get more attention from you as you compose your pages.

Alignment of display text

As type size gets larger, subtle differences among letters become more obvious. In prominent display text, the differences can create problems. Take a look at the illustration in Figure 6.26.

Figure 6.26 An example of display text where both lines actually have the same left margin—but it doesn't look that way.

Although the headline is left-aligned, it doesn't look that way. Round letters (*C, G, O, Q*) appear not to reach the left margin. To a lesser degree, the same will be true of slanted letters (*A, M, V, W*). So you should tweak your display text to correct this visual problem.

Notice the improvement in Figure 6.27.

Figure 6.27 Both lines now appear to have the same starting point.

Here, the first line, beginning with the round letter C, has been shifted slightly to the left to create an alignment that looks better.

Using quotation marks

In display text, quotation marks can create an unbalanced look. You can see the problem in Figure 6.28.

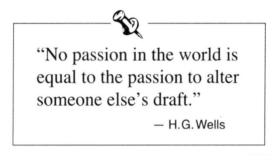

> "No passion in the world is equal to the passion to alter someone else's draft."
>
> — H.G. Wells

Figure 6.28 A block of display text that looks a little odd because of the opening quotation mark.

Although the text is set flush left, it looks awkward. A more attractive option is to use a hanging indent to offset the opening quotation mark so the text will be aligned. Notice the improvement in Figure 6.29.

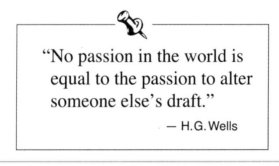

> "No passion in the world is equal to the passion to alter someone else's draft."
>
> — H.G. Wells

Figure 6.29 Hanging the opening quotation mark outside the left margin creates a better look.

With display text, the main concern should always be whether it *looks* correct, not whether it *is* correct.

Summary

Fine-tuning a page contributes to visual style when it eliminates unsightly visual problems that divert attention away from your message. Problems involving texture, patterns, direction, and association give pages an amateurish look and suggest carelessness. Being attentive to the ways text, space, and art interact will enable you to create pages that attract readers and get results. Fixing "minor" problems can make your work stand out from the crowd.

Afterword

AT FIRST, SOME OF YOUR publications will exude visual style and be attractive, understandable, and persuasive; others won't. To develop your sense of what works in print and what doesn't, you should make a habit of looking critically at every publication you see. Even the simplest documents often have a lesson to teach. Take, for example, a sign that was posted in a university library (Figure A.1).

What's wrong here? Just about everything. It's not visually pleasing. It's not very clear. And it's certainly not influential because it leaves readers unsure about what to do.

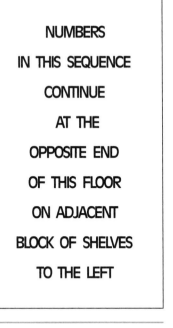

Figure A.1 An uninspired sign posted in the stacks of a university library.

Makeover

By applying a few of the simple techniques outlined in this book, we easily can make this sign more effective (Figure A.2). Notice the changes that were made to the original:

- The text was set in uppercase and lowercase letters.
- A serif typeface was used to make the text easier to read.
- A large initial letter was added to give emphasis and attract attention.
- The text alignment was changed from centered to justified to facilitate reading.
- The word *the* was added before *adjacent*.
- Leading was tightened to tie the text lines together.
- A diagram was added to clarify the message, enhance the visual appeal of the page, and make sure readers know what action to take.

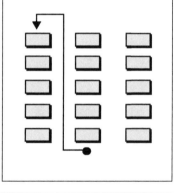

Figure A.2 An effective makeover that incorporates a few powerful techniques for improving visual appeal and clarity.

Learning to make good decisions about writing and design is not difficult. It's mostly a matter of gaining an awareness of the effect those decisions can have on readers. By continually looking for ways to apply the guidelines in this book, you'll gradually develop confidence and good judgment.

Glossary

Note: An asterisk (*) indicates a term not discussed in the book.

alignment   The shape of a block of text. It can be left-aligned (with a straight left edge), right-aligned (with a straight right edge), centered, or justified (with both edges straight).

art   Any graphic element other than conventional text or white space.

ascender   The part of a lowercase letter that extends above the x-height. The letters *b, d, f, h, k, l,* and *t* have ascenders. See also **x-height, descender**.

axis   An imaginary line on a page that helps in placing text and art elements to create a clear directionality.

balance   A design principle that stresses attention to the size, density, and apparent stability of graphic elements on a page.

baseline   The imaginary line on which letters sit. It creates the lower boundary of the type's x-height. See also **x-height**.

binding area*   An area on the inside edge of a page that allows for binding, created by shifting the text toward the outside edge.

bit-mapped image   A "paint" image comprising individual dots as opposed to geometric shapes. All scanned images are bit-mapped. Also called **raster image**. See also **vector image**.

bleed*   Art that extends beyond the margins to the edge of a page.

body text Any relatively long block of text, usually set in one typeface. See also **display text**.

bold A typeface style with thicker and darker letters than the normal style.

border A frame around text or art. Borders can range from simple lines to ornate cartouches.

bullet A character, such as ° or •, used to designate an item in a list.

call-out A word or phrase that identifies part of an illustration, often accompanied by an arrow.

caption The text that describes a figure, table, or illustration.

cliché* An overused word, phrase, image, or page layout that draws attention to itself by its familiarity.

clip art Stock image and designs that can be pasted into documents.

columns A format with text set in vertical sections. *Newspaper* columns allow text to "wrap" from the bottom of one column to the top of the next. *Parallel* columns are independent of one another.

continuity An organizational principle suggesting that comprehension is aided when there is a reasonable and predictable continuity in a message.

cropping Trimming rectangular portions from an image so it fits better into the context of a page. See also **masking**.

dash* See **em dash, en dash**.

descender The part of a lowercase letter that extends below the baseline. The letters *g*, *j*, *p*, *q*, and *y* have descenders. See also **baseline, ascender**.

diacritic* A mark on or near a letter that changes its usual pronunciation. Common diacritics in foreign-language words include the *tilde* (mañana), *acute accent* (cliché), *grave accent* (vis à vis), and *diaeresis* (über).

digitize To capture a printed image (with a scanner) or a scene (with a digital camera) as a digital file that can be used in publishing programs.

dingbat A small, simple graphic image such as ✤ or ➝.

display text A brief section of text such as a title, subheading, or ad copy. See also **body text**.

drop cap A large initial letter in body text that extends below the baseline of the text. See also **baseline, extended cap.**

drop shadow* A shadow on one or two sides of a box that gives a three-dimensional effect.

efficiency A measure that indicates how much text can fit into a given space. Typefaces with wide letters are less efficient than typefaces with narrow letters.

em* A unit of measure equal to the point size of the type being used. For example, in 12-point type, an em dash is 12 points wide. See also **em dash, en.**

em dash* A punctuation mark, one em wide, used to indicate a break in the flow of a sentence—like this. See also **em.**

en* A unit of measure equal to half an em. See also **en dash, em.**

en dash* A punctuation mark, one en wide, used to indicate a range. For example, A–Z, 1972–1976, 9:30–10:30. See also **en.**

extended cap A large initial letter in body text that extends above the text line. See also **drop cap.**

font A member of a typeface family, representing a particular combination of size and style. For example, Palatino 12-point bold is one font; Palatino 10-point italic is another. See also **typeface.**

footer A text line appearing at the bottom of each page. It's useful for showing page number, chapter title, date, and other information. See also **header.**

grid A structure of vertical and horizontal lines on a page—they don't print—that help in placing text and graphics in a balanced and consistent way.

gutter* The white space between two columns of text, or between two facing pages of text.

hanging indent A paragraph format wherein the first line begins at the left margin, and succeeding lines are indented.

harmony A design principle that stresses cohesiveness and unity of the various graphic elements on a page.

header A text line appearing at the top of each page. It's useful for showing page number, chapter title, date, and other information. See also **footer.**

index A list of a document's key words and topics, together with page number references.

initial cap See **extended cap**.

italic A serif type style that has a slanted and cursive appearance. See also **oblique, roman**.

jumpline A text line that indicates the continuation of an article on another page (for example, "See *Budget*, page 7").

justification The arrangement of text so both the left and right margins are straight.

kerning The process of adjusting the spacing of adjacent letters in display text to improve the appearance of words. See also **tracking**.

landscape A page oriented so that the width is greater than the height. See also **portrait**.

leader* A line, usually dotted, that guides the eye from one item to a related item.

leading Line or paragraph spacing.

letter spacing See **tracking**.

ligature* A printed character consisting of two joined letters. Common ligatures include *æ, fi,* and *fl.*

logo A company or product name designed to be eye-catching and distinctive.

lowercase Refers to non-capital letters.

macro A file containing a series of keystrokes, codes, and/or text. When you activate a macro, all of its operations are executed in sequence.

margin The area from the edge of a page to the text and art area.

masking Cutting out specific parts of an illustration that might be distracting. See also **cropping**.

masthead* A block of text in a newsletter that contains details about the staff, publisher, and subscriptions.

nameplate* A publication's name as it appears on the cover or front page of every issue.

oblique A sans serif type style that has a slanted appearance.

See also **italic**.

orphan   The first line of a paragraph that is stranded at the bottom of a page or column. See also **widow**.

paragraph leading   The space between paragraphs in body text.

pixel*   Short for *picture element*, an individual dot on a computer monitor.

point   A unit used to measure type and leading. There are approximately 72 points in an inch. See also **leading, typeface**.

portrait   A page oriented so that the height is greater than the width. See also **landscape**.

proportion   A design principle that takes into account the relative sizes and positions of graphic elements on a page.

proximity   An organizational principle that suggests that closeness helps to connect items logically.

pull-quote   A key portion of body text that is copied and presented prominently, often in larger type.

raised cap   See **extended cap**.

raster image   See **bit-mapped image**.

recto*   The right-side page. See also **verso**.

resolution   The fineness with which an image or text is represented.

reverse   Text that is set with white letters on a black background.

roman*   Conventional type that is vertical, as opposed to italic and oblique, which are slanted. See also **italic, oblique**.

rule   A line.

runaround   Text with a margin that follows the shape of an art element.

sans serif   A typeface without serifs; that is, the main strokes of the letters end abruptly. See also **serif**.

scanner   A device that converts a printed image to a digital image that can be manipulated in publishing programs.

screen   A shaded background on which text appears.

script   A typeface that simulates handwriting, calligraphy, or other irregular forms of printing.

sequence   A design principle that stresses attention to ingrained left-to-right and top-to-bottom reading patterns.

serif   A typeface with small strokes at the ends of the main strokes of the letters. See also **sans serif**.

silhouetting See **masking**.

similarity An organizational principle that suggests that similar ideas should be conveyed with similar language.

sink* The white space between the top of a page and the text.

small caps Uppercase letters that are only as tall as the x-height of the surrounding text, LIKE THIS. See also **x-height**.

space See **white space**.

spec sheet A reference page that shows particular type and leading combinations.

style A set of formatting codes that can be applied to recurring types of text—for example, subheadings.

symmetry The arrangement of graphic elements into a formal balance, usually about either a vertical or horizontal axis.

template A reusable "starter" document that's formatted with particular margins, typefaces, and other characteristics.

texture The overall appearance of a page resulting from the interaction of text, space, and art.

thumbnail sketch A small sketch showing a possible arrangement of text, space, and art for a page.

tombstoning The unintended alignment of subheadings in adjacent columns or on facing pages.

tracking The overall letter spacing throughout a word or phrase (in display text), or throughout a paragraph or page (in body text). See also **kerning**.

trim size* In commercial printing, the final size of a page after it is printed and cut.

typeface A family of related text styles and sizes. For example, Bookman 18-point, Bookman 8-point bold, and Bookman 10-point italic are members of the same typeface—Bookman. See also **font**.

type size The height of type, measured from the bottom of the longest descender to the top of the longest ascender.

type style A particular variation in the appearance of type—for example, outlined or shadowed.

typography The art of arranging type—and therefore space—on a page.

uppercase Capital letters.

vector image   A "draw" image comprising geometric objects instead of individual dots. Vector images can be easily rescaled without loss of resolution. See also **bit-mapped image**.

verso   The left-side page. See also **recto**.

white space   Any blank area on a page, regardless of the color of the paper.

widow   A short final line of a paragraph that is isolated at the top of a page or column. See also **orphan**.

x-height   The height of lowercase letters, excluding ascenders and descenders.

Sources
for Art and Fonts

Art Mania, Nova Development Corporation, Calabasas, CA, 1996.

Decorative Corners, Dover Publications, Mineola, NY, 1987.

Old-Fashioned Small Frames and Borders, Dover Publications, Mineola, NY, 1990.

The Print Shop Ensemble, Broderbund, Novato, CA, 1997.

Designed to a T (www.designedtoat.com).

Original drawings, designs, and photographs by the author.

Photographs by Liz Petersen.

Index

About the Author

AFTER EARNING DEGREES IN ART AND COGNITIVE Psychology, Robert W. Harris worked as a teacher during the 1980s. He has been a freelance writer and designer since 1990, authoring a dozen books that include the top-selling *DOS, WordPerfect & Lotus Office Companion* (Ventana Press), *When Good People Write Bad Sentences* (St. Martin's Press), and *101 Things NOT to Do Before You Die* (Thomas Dunne). His website is **www.rwhstudio.com.**